Contents

SECTION A

Widening horizons

The world has shrunk through cheaper air travel, and increased leisure and income allow ordinary people to travel to destinations that were once inaccessible. Two environments stand out as remaining mysterious and exotic. They are areas that few have directly experienced but only accessed through coffee table books, television programmes or films. The great rain forests and the hot deserts of the Tropics remain remote and hostile. To travel in them remains beyond the means and desire of most people. These are natural environments with few amenities; conditions are well beyond the comfort zone and require expedition-like organisation for any extended stay.

Figure 1.1 The Tropics as exotic

We know surprisingly little about the rain forests and deserts. Images from space have increased our knowledge, but our understanding of how they evolved and how they function remains incomplete. Attention has tended to focus on the bizarre and unusual, such as barchan dunes in deserts, the exotic fauna of the rain forest or the indigenous inhabitants (**1.1**), but much of the area classified as desert remains uncharted and the highly complex mechanisms of the rain forest remain partially studied. We know that the rain forest plays an important role in global atmospheric and hydrological systems and there is ever-growing concern about rates of deforestation. The hot deserts are also under threat from irrigated agriculture and colonisation.

TROPICAL

ENVIRONMENTS

Contrasting Regimes and Challenges

Richard Heelas

Series editor
Michael Witherick

Published in 2001 by:
Nelson Thornes Ltd
Delta Place
27 Bath Road
CHELTENHAM
GL53 7TH
United Kingdom

01 02 03 04 05 / 10 9 8 7 6 5 4 3 2 1

A catalogue record for this book is available from the British Library

ISBN 0 7487 5820 8

Illustrations and page make-up by Multiplex Techniques Ltd
Printed and bound in Great Britain by Ashford Colour Press

Acknowledgements
With thanks to the following for permission to reproduce photographs and other
copyright material in this book:

Philip Allen Publishers, *Geography Review*, Volume 13, Number 5, May 2000,
Fig 3.5; Australian Tourist Commission, Figs 1.1, 5.1; Corbis, Fig 3.2, 4.4;
Corel, Figs 5.2, 5.4, 5.5, 6.5; Richard Heelas, 8.1; Christopher Pillitz/Network,
Fig 8.5; Dick Roberts Photo Library, Fig 4.1; David Waugh, Fig 8.6; SSEC
Wisconsin University, Fig 2.3.

Every effort has been made to contact copyright holders. The publishers
apologise to anyone whose rights have been inadvertently overlooked, and will be
happy to rectify any errors or omissions.

Despite this, our concern about these environments remains peripheral. There is a tacit feeling that they are too large and too hostile really to disappear. Remoteness from the developed countries of the temperate world acts as a filter to active involvement. Issues of gene pools, global warming, the fate of indigenous people, aridity and drought are common themes in the media, but it is difficult to relate to events that are occurring so far away and in such different environments.

The Tropics are lines of latitude, 23°N (Tropic of Cancer) and 23°S (Tropic of Capricorn) of the Equator. Strictly speaking, the term 'Tropics' refers to the zone within these latitudes, but more generally it includes a wider belt extending 30° from the Equator. This belt receives a net gain of solar radiation that produces either higher than average rainfall (the rain forests) or conditions of extreme aridity (the deserts). It contains some of the wettest and driest environments in the world, as well as some of the highest and lowest population densities.

Review

1 Find out what parts of the Tropics are established destinations for tourists from the UK. What are their attractions?

In this book, three tropical environments will be examined: the hot deserts (dry all year), semi-arid environments (with a dominant dry season) and the tropical humid environments (wet all year). Although sharing spatial proximity, these environments offer stark contrasts and great variety. In terms of landforms, hydrology, soils, vegetation and events, these are regions of excess, often representing the extreme of global patterns. The indigenous populations have retained primitive cultures through the 20th century but, at the start of the new millennium, the future of the tropical forests and deserts remains very much in doubt.

SECTION B

Tropical climates

Figure 1.2 The climates of the Tropics (after Köppen): see the text for an explanation of the areas of interest

Climate refers to a statistical average of temperature, precipitation, evaporation and winds over a large area and a significant period of time (usually 35 years). The general distribution of climatic types in the Tropics is shown in **1.2**, a modification of the Köppen classification. While there is some latitudinal pattern, the main zones appear as cells, generally corresponding to the distribution of land and sea.

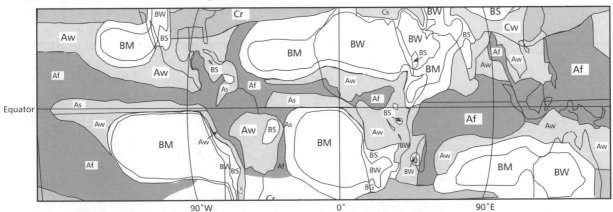

Review

2 Define the following terms:

- **climate**

- **the Tropics**

- **classification**.

3 Referring to **1.2**, describe:

- the distribution of arid (BW) regions

- how the distribution pattern differs from that of the Af regions.

4 Explain how and why arid climates (BM) can occur over oceans.

Desert climates (BW and BM)   These are areas with a marked water deficit; the annual loss of water through evapotranspiration is greater than the gain of water from precipitation. Over land masses (BW), this is sufficient to limit vegetation, while over the oceans (BM) evaporation is significantly higher than precipitation. In the Southern Hemisphere, there are three main cells of aridity extending inland from the west coasts of South America, Africa and Australia. These are the Atacama, Kalahari and Great Australian Deserts respectively. In the Northern Hemisphere, North America and North Africa show a similar pattern with the Californian and Sahara deserts, but in Asia the Gobi Desert extends to almost 50°N.

Semi-arid climates (BS)   In the Köppen classification, these are termed **steppe** climates and are characterised by distinctive arid and humid seasons. In addition, precipitation is generally infrequent and unreliable, so that periods of water surplus may be followed by extended drought. Total rainfall is relatively high (in north-east Brazil it averages over 900 mm) but it is poorly distributed and often lost rapidly through high rates of run-off and evapotranspiration. This climate occurs in Central USA, north-east Brazil, the Sahel in Africa and in southern Russia and western China. It often forms transition areas around true deserts.

Humid topical climates (Af)   These climatic regimes are wet all year and have no clear dry season. Total annual rainfall is generally over 2000 mm and this coincides with low evaporation. The result is a water surplus for most of the year and an abundance of vegetation. The climate forms a fairly regular zone, straddling the Equator between 10°N and 10°S, and includes much of the lowland Amazon Basin, the Congo Basin in Africa and the islands of South-East Asia.

Tropical heat

The Tropics receive high levels of solar radiation throughout the year and, in terms of systems, have a net energy gain. At the Equator, the Sun is overhead at noon twice a year (21 March and 21 September), these dates being known as the **equinoxes**. The Sun is overhead at the Tropic of Cancer on 21 June and at the Tropic of Capricorn on 21 December (the **solstices**). The reason for this movement is that the Earth's axis is not in alignment with that of the Sun, causing a seasonal shift in temperature zones. The angle of inclination of the Sun's rays is important, as it determines heat intensity and thus the extent of surface heating. At the Equator, the level of solar radiation is always high, but with increasing latitude there is an increase in seasonality in terms of day length and temperature. Throughout the Tropics, there is a net annual gain of radiation, and it is this that unifies the diverse climates of the zone (**1.3**).

Solar radiation is mainly in the form of short-wave energy, which is reduced as it passes through the atmosphere by:

- reflection from clouds
- scattering by solid materials
- absorption by water.

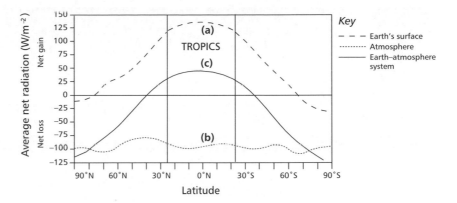

Figure 1.3 Variations in the average annual net radiation gain or loss by latitude: **(a)** by the Earth's surface; **(b)** by the atmosphere; **(c)** by the Earth's surface and the atmosphere taken together

On average, only 51 per cent of the energy received at the outer atmosphere (the **solar constant**) reaches the surface. At the Earth's surface, short-wave energy is either reflected (determined by the **albedo**) or it is absorbed into the ground, to be released as long-wave energy. It is the long-wave radiation that heats the atmosphere above the Earth's surface. Points on the same latitude receive the same amount of solar radiation at the outer atmosphere (the solar constant), but the amount of heat absorbed by the surface varies significantly from place to place. This is due to variations in the amount of energy lost in the atmosphere, whether the surface is land or water and its albedo (**1.4**).

Figure 1.4 The energy balance

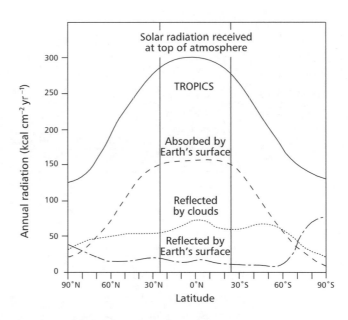

Temperatures in the Tropics are high, but stations show considerable variation due not only to latitude but also to altitude and proximity to the sea. Figure **1.5** illustrates the temperature patterns at both 'typical' and some more unusual stations.

Temperature (°C) and rainfall (mm)	J	F	M	A	M	J	J	A	S	O	N	D	Total
Typical stations													
Manaus (tropical humid)													
Mean monthly temp.	28	28	28	27	28	28	28	29	29	29	29	28	28
Daily maximum temp.	31	31	31	31	31	31	32	33	34	32	33	32	32
Daily minimum temp.	24	24	24	24	24	24	24	24	24	25	25	24	24
Rainfall	279	278	300	287	193	99	61	41	62	112	165	220	2096
Alice Springs (hot desert)													
Mean monthly temp.	28	27	25	20	15	12	12	14	18	23	25	27	21
Daily maximum temp.	35	35	32	27	23	19	19	23	27	31	33	35	28
Daily minimum temp.	21	20	17	12	8	5	4	6	10	15	18	20	13
Rainfall	44	33	27	10	15	13	7	8	7	18	29	38	249
Timbuktu (semi-arid)													
Mean monthly temp.	22	25	28	31	34	34	32	30	31	31	28	23	29
Daily maximum temp.	31	35	38	41	43	42	38	35	38	40	37	31	37
Daily minimum temp.	13	16	18	22	26	27	25	24	24	23	18	14	21
Rainfall	0	0	0	1	4	20	54	93	31	3	0	0	206
Less typical stations													
Quito (tropical humid)													
Mean monthly temp.	15	15	15	15	15	14	14	15	15	15	15	15	15
Daily maximum temp.	22	22	22	21	21	22	22	23	23	22	22	22	22
Daily minimum temp.	8	9	9	9	9	7	7	7	7	8	7	8	8
Rainfall	119	131	154	185	130	54	20	25	81	134	96	104	1233
Antofagasta (desert)													
Mean monthly temp.	21	21	20	18	16	15	15	14	15	16	18	19	17
Daily maximum temp.	25	25	24	21	20	19	17	17	18	19	21	22	21
Daily minimum temp.	17	17	16	15	13	11	11	11	12	13	15	16	14
Rainfall	0	0	0	1	1	3	5	3	1	1	1	0	18
Quixeramobim, north-east Brazil (semi-arid)													
Mean monthly temp.	29	28	27	27	27	26	27	28	28	29	29	29	28
Rainfall	42	121	209	173	118	58	16	5	6	3	4	10	769

Figure 1.5 Climate at typical and unusual tropical stations

- **Manaus** (3°S) experiences a low seasonal variation in temperature and a low diurnal range. The mean monthly temperature range is 2° and the greatest difference between the daily maximum and minimum is 10° in September.
- **Alice Springs** (23°S) has an average mean monthly temperature range of 16° and the greatest diurnal range is 17° in August and September.
- **Timbuktu** (17°N) has a mean average monthly temperature range of 17° and the greatest diurnal range is 19° in February, March and April.

Atmospheric circulation and precipitation

When air is heated, it becomes less dense and tends to rise; this process is termed **instability** or **convection**. Heating at the Equator produces a belt of rising air that forms a dominant feature of the global atmospheric circulatory system. This highly complex system is often simplified as a three-cell system, known as the tricellular circulation model (**1.6**).

Figure 1.6 The tricellular circulation model

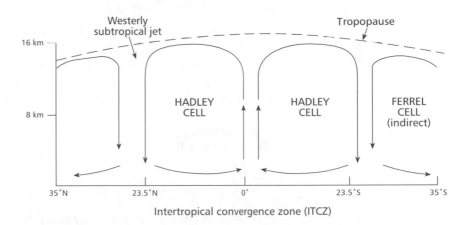

The ascending branch of the Hadley cell is caused by the intense heating of the Earth's surface. There is sufficient energy to push the atmosphere outwards to over 16 km (the **tropopause**). In the upper atmosphere, the air has cooled and spreads towards the poles. At between 20° and 30° N and S, cold air sinks towards the surface, forming the descending branches of the Hadley and Ferrel cells. The descending air heats up, but the mass of colder air above is sufficient to maintain descent until the air flows outwards at the surface. The locations of the cells move in a seasonal pattern. In June the rising branch of the Hadley cell is to the north of the Equator, in December to the south and in March and September over the Equator.

Water in the atmosphere is derived from evapotranspiration at the surface. The global hydrological cycle is a closed system, and if some regions receive more than the average rainfall then other regions must receive less. This basic system is most evident in the Tropics, where parts of northern India receive more than their fair share, with over a staggering 25 000 mm a year, while in the Atacama Desert of Peru and Chile rainfall is negligible.

Why these extremes occur owes much to the changes in the characteristics of air as it circulates in the Hadley cell.

The convergence of the ascending branches of the Hadley cells forms an area of low pressure (**1.6**) that is generally clearly evident on satellite images as a latitudinal belt of cloud. The processes responsible for the formation of this cloud and rain are discussed in **Chapter 4**. The descending branches of the Hadley and Ferrel cells are also evident in satellite images as large – often circular – areas, devoid of cloud. These are areas of high pressure (or **anticyclones**) and the processes occurring in these systems are examined in **Chapter 2**.

The areas between the rising and descending branches of the Hadley cell experience both high- and low-pressure conditions during the course of a year. In areas where this alternation is relatively balanced and reliable, climates with defined dry and wet seasons occur (Köppen Aw climates). But where the high-pressure systems still tend to dominate, semi-arid climates occur (see **Chapter 3**).

Climate is a very important part of the environment in which people live. It controls the geomorphological processes that shape the surface, the formation of soils, the nature of vegetation cover and the availability of water. All aspects of our lives are affected by climate and, even with high technology, it can still pose a threat to life and well-being through hazards.

Review

5 How does the angle of inclination of solar radiation affect the temperature at the Earth's surface?

6 What is meant by an **energy surplus**?

7 How is energy transferred from regions of net gain to regions of net loss?

8 What is meant by the term **albedo**?

9 Why is more energy reflected by the Earth's surface in the Tropics of the Northern Hemisphere than in the South (**1.4**)?

10 Using **1.5**, describe the main differences between tropical humid and tropical arid climates in terms of monthly and diurnal temperature ranges.

11 Try to explain why the highest maximum temperatures are not necessarily at the Equator.

12 Sketch a graph to compare mean monthly temperatures at Manaus and Quito.

Potential and constraints

The Tropics have great potential. High solar radiation provides one of the basic requirements for life and the tropical rain forests are the most productive of the global ecosystems. With high temperatures and an absence of seasons, photosynthesis is extremely high and capable of supporting high-yielding agriculture. In the past, important civilisations have emerged in these regions, including the Maya of Central America, the Incas of the Andes, the civilisations of Egypt and Jordan, as well as those of Thailand and Burma. Where the desert has been irrigated and made to 'bloom', agriculture has flourished and the landscape transformed. In the humid Tropics of the Far East, the development of plantation agriculture has demonstrated the high agricultural potential. In addition, tropical regions contain considerable mineral reserves, including bauxite, cassiterite, copper, precious stones and metals, as well as oil, gas and salt. Oil reserves in the Gulf have supported extensive urban and industrial development, transforming initially harsh environments into urban landscapes.

At the same time, however, the very abundance of energy creates a hostile environment, characterised by extremes that people have struggled to control and exploit in a systematic and sustainable manner. In the humid Tropics, with both heat and precipitation, the scale of the biodiversity is mirrored by the prevalence of pests, bacteria and viruses, as well as natural hazards including storms and landslides. Micro-organisms affect the health of crops and people; malaria, yellow fever, cholera and typhoid remain endemic in many regions. Soils and biomass have proved remarkably fragile and difficult to exploit. In deserts, with heat but little precipitation, vegetation and fauna struggle to survive, and such regions can only support sparse and often nomadic populations without the provision of water. Existing on the edge of survival, these ecosystems are extremely fragile to any additional stress, making sustainable exploitation difficult.

Some insight into why these regions are sparsely populated is possible through reference to **comfort zones** (1.7). These relate climate to human activity. For Europeans, the humid and dry Tropics lie well outside the comfort zone, reducing the attractiveness of such areas for colonisation.

Review

13 Do you think that tropical climate is the only factor behind the 'hostility' of the rain forest and the desert?

14 Explain why 'heat' is a potential for human activity.

15 Attempt to explain the significance of comfort zones.

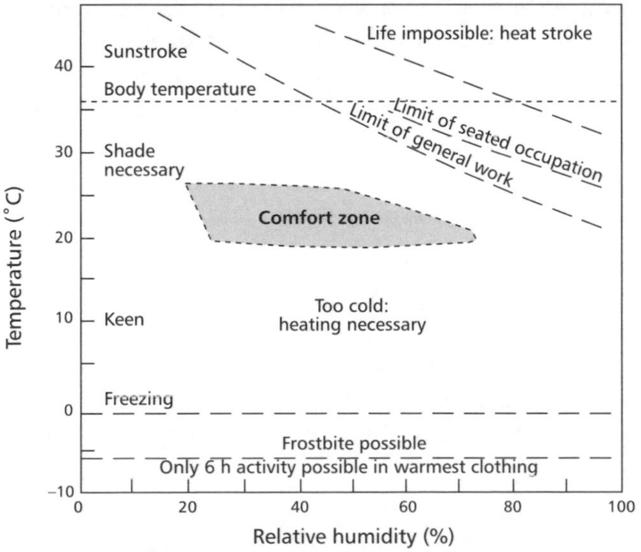

Figure 1.7
Comfort zones

Why are the Tropics an issue?

Until the 20th century, the Tropics were regarded as exotic environments, visited and exploited by the adventurous but indestructible in their immensity and hostility. They provided a source of exotic images, bizarre customs, strange stories and unusual foods and materials. Migration from, and investment by, the Old World into the New World focused on environments more akin to those back home, such as south-east Brazil, South Africa or the plains of India. As a consequence, the expanses of tropical rain forest and desert were largely ignored. In Brazil, early attempts to exploit the tropical rain forest including natural rubber failed, increasing the perception that such environments could not be productive.

With development limited, much of the tropical forest and desert retained its indigenous populations, who continued to follow a traditional way of life well into the 20th century. This was not a result of any policy decision but, rather, a consequence of the land not being wanted. These areas are now termed **wilderness regions**, and are characterised by a lack of development and population. Four main areas of wilderness remain:

- tropical rain forests – in South America, Africa and parts of the Far East
- hot desert regions – in South America, parts of North America, Africa, the Middle East, Asia and Australia
- cold deserts – in Greenland, North America, the Arctic and Antarctica
- mountain areas – including North and South America, Northern Europe, Asia and the Middle East.

During the 20th century, the pressure on land and resources increased, and these once sparsely inhabited areas are under threat. This is due to both accelerating population growth in tropical countries, fuelled by decreasing death rates, and the increased global demand for resources and food. In addition, developments in technology have encouraged attempts to control, manage and exploit the more hostile environments, as confidence grows that humans can overcome nature. A growing awareness of the environment has resulted in a questioning of the nature of progress and demands for sustainability and conservation. This has placed the Tropics in the front line of the battle between groups that want economic development and those determined that the last remaining virgin areas of the planet should remain untouched.

So, to sum up, the Tropics form a diverse region unified by high rates of solar radiation but divided by patterns of precipitation. In rain forests and hot deserts, the zone contains two of the most unusual natural environments, which are under increasing pressure from development. The Tropics look set to play a more important role in the 21st century, as much of their human and physical potential has yet to be realised.

16 What is meant by the term **indigenous culture**?

17 Of the four types of wilderness region, which one do you think is most threatened? Give your reasons and be sure to identify the specific threats.

Enquiry

1 a Construct a line graph to show the monthly mean temperature for Manaus and Alice Springs (**1.5**).
  b Using an alternative technique and an appropriate scale, plot the data for precipitation on to the same graph.
  c Attempt to explain the differences in temperature that are evident on the graph.
  d Use an appropriate statistical technique (at a 0.05 per cent confidence level) to determine if there is a relationship between mean monthly temperature and precipitation at Alice Springs. Suggest reasons for the relationship that you have noted.

2 a Use the Internet to search for a recent image of global water vapour. Copy the image, either as a sketch or a printout.
  b Using an atlas, locate the Equator and the Tropics of Capricorn and Cancer on the image. Describe the pattern of water vapour in the Tropics.
  c With reference to one continent, describe the extent to which the pattern of water vapour corresponds with the pattern of forest and desert.
  d To what extent can the influence of ocean currents on atmospheric water vapour be seen on your image?

Hot desert processes

Definitions and delimitation

When it comes to discussing tropical arid environments, a number of key terms enter the vocabulary. Perhaps it would be helpful to start by clarifying what each means.

- **Deserts** are areas characterised by sparse or absent vegetation cover, so that the surface is directly exposed to atmospheric processes. This is generally associated with a low total or extremely irregular precipitation (**hot deserts**) but may also be caused by very low temperatures (**cold deserts**). This term refers to biogeography as much as to climate, and areas cease to be considered as 'desert' after successful irrigation or colonisation.
- **Aridity** is a climatic term referring to those areas that receive less than 250 mm of rainfall a year. The term implies a net water deficit, with potential evaporation in excess of precipitation.
- **Semi-arid areas** have a low or irregular pattern of precipitation. Equally, they may have an extended dry season that inhibits the growth of vegetation. Precipitation is greater than 250 mm a year, but there is a water deficit due to high rates of evapotranspiration or high rates of surface run-off.
- **Dry land** is a general term used to refer to areas classified as arid, semi-arid and dry savanna (Aw on **1.2**), that cover approximately 36 per cent of the Earth's surface – and reach 82 per cent in the driest continent, Australia. These are areas where the mean annual precipitation is less than potential evapotranspiration, creating an annual water deficit.
- **Drought** is a period of dryness that represents a significant deviation from the average pattern of rainfall. It leads to a depletion of soil water and groundwater and adversely affects the natural vegetation. In the UK, it refers to any period of more than 15 days with no day receiving more than 0.2 mm of precipitation. In arid areas, where average rainfall is extremely low, the concept of drought can only be applied to extremely long dry periods.

When it comes to measures of dryness, perhaps one of the most widely used is the **moisture index**. This quantifies the relationship between precipitation (input) and evapotranspiration (output). The index value ranges from – 100 (when precipitation is zero) to +100 (when precipitation greatly exceeds evapotranspiration). An index value of – 40 is taken as the threshold between arid and semi-arid regions, and a value of – 20 marks the beginning of semi-aridity.

Figure 2.1 Peltier's delineation of morphogenetic regions

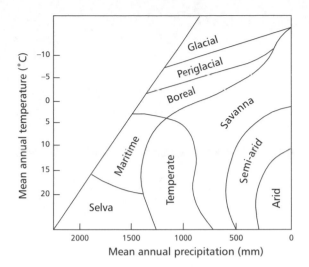

Review

1 In your own words, attempt to explain the difference between **aridity** and **desert**.

2 Why is total precipitation of limited use in defining a **desert**?

Classifications of physical environments tend to be based either on vegetation (desert) or on climatic data (arid and semi-arid). Climatic data, such as are used in **2.1**, suggest that an accurate delineation of climatic zones and their associated **morphogenetic** regions is possible. In reality, such divisions are difficult to justify, as climates gradually merge from one type to another. It is important to bear in mind the existence of these continuums, and that each climatic type and its associated physical environment have, as it were, a 'core' and a 'periphery'.

SECTION B

Causes of aridity and heat

Above the Tropics, the air that has cooled during ascent from the intertropical convergence zone (ITCZ) collects in the upper atmosphere as a highly stable and very cold mass (**1.6**). Near the tropopause, the westerly tropical jet streams modify the position of this convergence, and thereby determine the location and strength of the descending branch of the Hadley cell. As the cold air descends, it is compressed to form high-pressure (anticyclonic) systems. It also heats up adiabatically. Since, during its prior ascent, the air has lost its moisture through cloud and rain formation, it heats up at the dry adiabatic lapse rate (DALR) of 1°C per 100 m. Heating increases the water-bearing capacity and this causes a decrease in relative humidity. The air cannot rise, as the mass of cold air above forces the lower air downwards, and this creates highly stable atmospheric conditions (**2.2**). With decreasing relative humidity, the remaining water vapour in the air is unable to condense. This results in sparse cloud cover and low rainfall (**2.3**).

Figure 2.2 Atmospheric stability

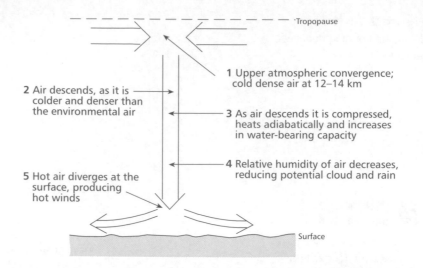

- - - - - - - - - - - - Tropopause

1 Upper atmospheric convergence; cold dense air at 12–14 km

2 Air descends, as it is colder and denser than the environmental air

3 As air descends it is compressed, heats adiabatically and increases in water-bearing capacity

4 Relative humidity of air decreases, reducing potential cloud and rain

5 Hot air diverges at the surface, producing hot winds

Surface

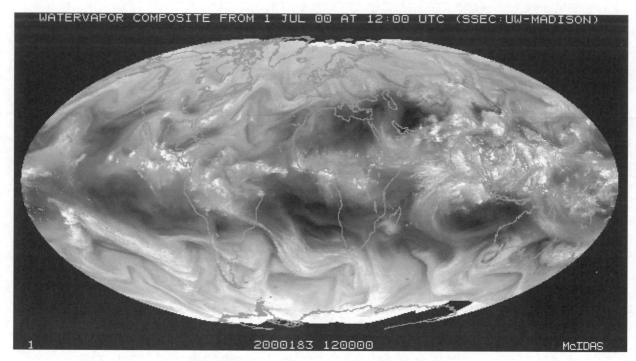

WATERVAPOR COMPOSITE FROM 1 JUL 00 AT 12:00 UTC (SSEC:UW-MADISON)

1   2000183 120000   McIDAS

Figure 2.3 Global water vapour

The low latitude of between 15 and 30° gives a high angle of inclination to short-wave energy from the Sun. This is enhanced by the absence of cloud to absorb and reflect energy. Surfaces heat up rapidly during the day but cool rapidly at night, giving a large diurnal temperature range. However, not all tropical deserts are extremely hot, as the absence of vegetation can be influenced by other factors, including cold ocean currents. This helps to explain the west coast distribution of deserts between 15 and 30°, including the Atacama, Kalahari and southern Californian deserts and, to some extent, the Sahara.

Ocean currents form a global circulatory system. In low latitudes, cold surface water cools the overlying air, causing an inversion and local

Figure 2.4 The Atacama
– cold ocean currents and
aridity

atmospheric stability. As the offshore air is cooled it sinks, condenses and forms sea fogs or mists adjacent to the coast. This prevents the warm, moist maritime air from flowing over the coastal area. In effect, the offshore cold current blocks the potentially rain-bearing air from the coastal zone (**2.4**).

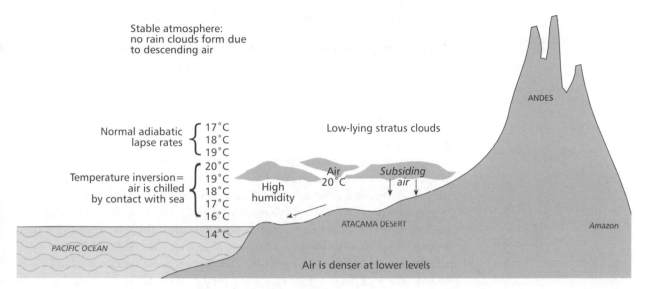

Cold ocean currents are part of the global circulation caused by the difference in temperature and density of the oceans. Water is densest at 4°C, so that polar water tends to sink and move towards the Equator. This displaces water heated in the Tropics, which moves towards the Poles as less dense surface flows. The Coriolis force, generated by the rotation of the Earth, gives a clockwise surface circulation in the Northern Hemisphere and an anti-clockwise one in the Southern Hemisphere. The scale of some cold currents is increased by the topography of the sea floor and, in particular, by ocean trenches – as off the coasts of North and South America – which helps to explain the prevalence of west coast deserts.

Review

3 Explain what is meant by the following:

■ relative humidity
■ an adiabatic process
■ atmospheric stability.

4 Why are cloud and rain less likely as air descends through the atmosphere?

5 How do cold ocean currents block on-shore winds?

6 Select one west coast desert, and identify the adjacent cold ocean current and the prevailing wind direction.

Weathering and mass movement

In this section and the next two, the focus is on those processes responsible for the landforms that are regarded as typical of hot deserts.

Weathering

Weathering is the breakdown, disintegration and decay of rock *in situ* through mechanical, chemical and biological processes, producing a layer, or mantle, of debris termed 'regolith'. This unconsolidated material has a low resistance and can be removed by mass movement and erosion. In arid regions, rates of weathering are generally low due to the low precipitation, but despite this it is still valid to distinguish between **mechanical** (physical) and **chemical weathering**.

Insolation weathering is an important mechanical processes. The high inclination of the Sun and the absence of cloud cover cause high diurnal ranges of surface temperatures. During the day, rock surfaces heat, expand and pull away from the cooler core. At night, with the rapid radiation of long-wave energy, the rock surface cools rapidly, causing the outer shell to crack around the larger core. With repeated cycles, this causes spherical weathering or **exfoliation** (the rock literally peels like skin). This was thought to be particularly important on heterogeneous rocks, such as granite, where different minerals expanded and contracted at different rates. However, attempts to demonstrate this under laboratory conditions have been largely unsuccessful.

Recent research has suggested that disintegration through the pressure of **salt crystal growth** is a common process in arid regions. Alkaline groundwater is drawn towards the surface by capillary action and evaporates. In permeable and porous rocks, individual gains are forced apart (**granular disintegration**); while in pervious rocks, cleavage into angular debris is more common (**block disintegration**).

During denudation, the pressure on underlying rocks is progressively reduced, causing cracks to open. This **pressure release** is particularly common in igneous rocks (including granite) and in folded or faulted structures. The cracks increase perviousness and are enlarged by other weathering processes. Infrequent precipitation penetrates into rocks, causing them to expand, particularly in the case of clays. Subsequent evaporation causes water loss and shrinkage, which generate pressures that bring about cracking and disintegration.

Chemical weathering processes involve a chemical modification to the rock and it is now thought that these are important in desert regions. **Hydration** is a chemical reaction that involves a mineral combining with a water molecule and expanding. This exerts pressure on surrounding material and the rock disintegrates. Hydration does not require acidic water and it is not affected by evaporation, as the water becomes part of the mineral. This process is increasingly seen as important in arid areas.

Carbonation and **hydrolysis** require an acidic solution to react with minerals and, as groundwater and soil water in arid regions are generally alkaline, carbonation and hydrolysis generally have a very low intensity and a localised distribution. **Oxidation** involves a reaction between atmospheric oxygen and iron compounds in the soil or rock that causes decay and disintegration. Water is required and this is an important form of weathering in sandstone.

Water containing minerals in solution rises to the surface by capillary action, leading to the accumulation of minerals at the surface. **Desert varnish** is a thin veneer of iron and manganese oxides on surface pebbles and rocks, and can form rapidly if groundwater is available. A thicker and more extensive mineral accumulation at the surface is termed **duricrust**, and these resistant surfaces of laterite, silcrete, calcrete and gypcrete possibly owe their origin to pervious, more humid, climates.

Finally, it needs to be emphasised that there remains considerable controversy over the nature of weathering processes in arid regions. There is a growing recognition of the importance of crystal growth and hydration, as well as the role of water in seemingly dry areas. What is agreed is that weathering rates are relatively low and that rates vary considerably within arid areas depending on groundwater availability. This helps to explain the great variation in topography found in arid regions.

Mass movement

Mass movement is the localised transfer of regolith, rock or soil downslope under the influence of gravity. It occurs when the stress force operating on a slope is greater than the cohesive and frictional forces holding the material in place. Mass movement is a system in **dynamic equilibrium**. Thus a steepening of the angle increases the stress force, causing the slope to fail. This in turn reduces the angle and stress force and creates a new stable slope. Precipitation is a major factor, as it both increases the stress force on slopes by adding weight and decreases cohesive and frictional forces through dissolving mineral cements and through lubricating the contact zones between particles. In deserts, slopes can be maintained at steep angles, as mass movement is limited (**2.5a**). Slope form is often determined by the size of particles (repose slopes), as slopes are produced when moving particles come to rest. In general, the larger the particle, the greater is the slope angle. It is this that accounts for the frequency of steep debris slopes in arid regions.

During and immediately after periods of heavy rain, the intensity of mass movement increases. When dry, regolith supports stable slopes, but as soon as those slopes are wettened, they suddenly become mobile, giving rise to mudslides, rock streams and debris flows that radically modify the landscape. This alternation, of long periods of relative stability interrupted by infrequent and unpredictable bursts of activity, is a characteristic of processes in arid areas.

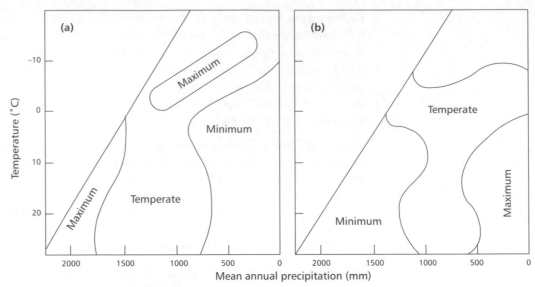

Figure 2.5
Peltier's diagrams of (**a**) mass movement and (**b**) aeolian processes

Review

7 Explain why rates of weathering are slow in arid regions.

8 What evidence could be used to assess rates of weathering in arid areas?

9 What other factors could account for the shallow depth of regolith in arid areas?

10 Write a brief account highlighting the essential features shown by **2.5a** and explain what the diagram conveys about mass movement in hot deserts.

Aeolian processes

Erosion is the removal, transport and subsequent modification of material by an external source of energy. In arid regions the two main processes are wind (aeolian) and water (fluvial).

Wind is the movement of air horizontally to the surface as a response to a pressure gradient. The energy is derived from solar radiation that heats air, changing its density, and causes it to rise (convection) and subside. Surface winds are a compensatory movement, with flows from high- to low-pressure systems (**1.6**). In the Tropics, the main wind systems are the 'Trades', which flow from the sub-tropical anticyclones towards the equatorial low. The Trades do not flow directly from high to low pressure, but are deflected by the rotation of the Earth, the Coriolis effect, forming the North-East Trades in the Northern Hemisphere and the South-West Trades in the Southern Hemisphere (**geostrophic winds**). In low latitudes, these systems and associated winds are relatively strong and persistent, increasing the potential of aeolian processes.

Air has a low mass and this reduces its effectiveness as an agent of erosion. In addition, its flow characteristics are easily disrupted, decreasing velocity and energy. Over flat surfaces, in particular the sea, air flows in laminar sheets, with increasing velocity at increasing altitude. Air at the surface is slowed by external friction and obstructions cause turbulence, breaking up the laminar flow and increasing internal friction. In arid areas, the sparseness of vegetation reduces turbulence and increases the effectiveness of aeolian erosion.

The reasons why wind is more important in deserts than in other environments are as follows:

- Strong anticyclones and deep lows produce steep pressure gradients.
- The pressure systems are persistent, producing strong prevailing winds.
- In coastal areas wind speed is high due to low turbulence.
- There is an absence of vegetation to reduce surface wind speed.
- The surface is generally dry, reducing the weight of particles.
- Other agents of erosion are weak, as it is too dry for fluvial processes and too warm for glaciation.

Wind transports material in three main ways:

- suspension
- saltation
- surface creep.

The balance of these processes depends on a combination of wind speed, the angle of slope, particle size and particle density. To be effective, wind speeds must generally be above 25 kph and maintain a constant direction.

Suspension

Very fine particles (< 0.1 mm in diameter) are lifted from the surface and moved upwards into faster-moving air. These particles are predominantly clays, silts and fine sand. The critical wind speed required to start to move surface material is termed the **fluid threshold**. Once this has been reached, the whole surface becomes active and fine material is lifted into the faster airflow above the surface. The velocity at which deposition occurs is termed the **impact threshold** and this is generally lower than the fluid threshold. There is some evidence that very fine particles (< 0.05 mm diameter) have higher fluid thresholds, as their high surface area to mass ratio causes adhesion and sticking. Suspended load can be transported for considerable distances. In 1984, El-Baz estimated that between 25 and 37 million tonnes a year of suspended material is transported through longitude 60°W. The load is mainly concentrated in dust clouds at between 1.5 and 3.7 km altitude. In the local source area, suspended load may form choking dust storms, and in areas of deposition the material forms loess or brickearth (although such deposits may originate from periglacial areas as well as hot deserts). At infrequent intervals (approximately once every ten years) Saharan sand is deposited in south-west and southern England.

Saltation

Particles of between 0.1 and 1.0 mm in diameter are too heavy to be lifted into the upper air, but they can be lifted locally up to 2 m. In strong winds, these particles rise almost vertically, before returning to the ground in a more gentle trajectory. In storms, the 1 m layer above the surface becomes active with material in saltation, as particles leapfrog each other in a downwind direction. Attempts to study saltation have included long-term exposure of rods and blocks to desert winds (one experiment by Sharp has been running for over 11 years). By recording changes to the surface of the rods, Sharp came to the conclusion that abrasion by saltation was greatest at 23 cm above the surface. Later research placed the zone a little lower, at 10–15 cm. This zone of maximum effect is where particles are already in movement and in strong wind above surface turbulence.

Surface creep

Particles in saltation collide with surface particles, slowly pushing them in a downwind direction. This can move particles above 1.0 mm diameter, and observations suggest that on glazed surfaces particles as heavy as 50 g can creep upslope under winds of 60–75 kph.

The progressive removal of material by wind is termed **deflation**. The **competence** of wind (that is, the weight of the largest particles that an agent of erosion can pick up and transport) is relatively low, so that only finer clays and silts are generally removed. The effectiveness depends on the calibre of the material available, and this depends on the lithology, rates of weathering and the origin of the surface material.

Is wind important?

The availability of detailed satellite images has helped to re-establish the importance of aeolian erosion (**2.5b**). Images of the Tibesti Massif in the Sahara clearly show large-scale grooves between 0.5 and 1 km wide, running in alignment with the prevailing wind. These shallow valley systems are regularly spaced between 0.5 and 2 km apart and dominate the landscape over 90 000 km^2 (**2.6**). Major depressions in desert regions also appear to have been excavated by wind action, as their floors lie well below base level. The Qattara Depression in Egypt lies 134 m below sea level, and it is estimated that 3300 km^3 of material has been removed, mainly by aeolian erosion. In the Kalahari Desert there are over 9000 depressions and many of these show wind orientation. Many depressions fill with water after heavy rain to form shallow lakes (**playas**), increasing rates of chemical and mechanical weathering, and providing finer regolith to be removed in suspension. In contrast, the surrounding uplands are drier and weather less rapidly, increasing the contrast in relief.

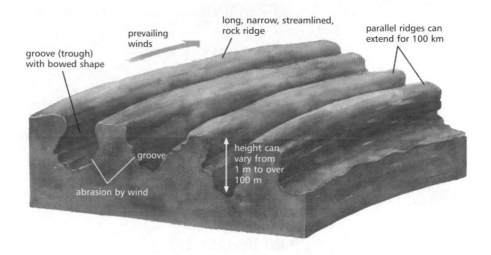

Figure 2.6 Formation of wind-shaped valleys

prevailing winds

long, narrow, streamlined, rock ridge

parallel ridges can extend for 100 km

groove (trough) with bowed shape

groove

abrasion by wind

height can vary from 1 m to over 100 m

Desert or **stone pavements** extend over large areas and are termed **reg** in North Africa or **gibber plains** in Australia. These relatively bare surfaces consist of cobble-sized material, one or two stones thick, often closely packed into a durable surface, and lie over material of finer texture as a protective layer. These are thought to be a product of deflation, with the larger stones accumulating at the surface as the finer material is removed by the wind and then protecting the underlying fine material from further aeolian erosion. Alternative explanations for stone pavements include sorting by fluvial processes, either in the past or during present-day storms, or vertical sorting through the processes of wetting and drying. The latter appear to be particularly important on Australian gibber plains, where changes in humidity produce patterned ground.

Strange sculptured landforms, including yardangs and zeugens, also demonstrate aeolian processes. **Yardangs** are ridges, often showing aerodynamic shaping with a blunt windward end and tapering on the downwind end. Yardangs may extend for over 100 km (as in Tibesti) and occur on both unconsolidated surfaces and more resistant sedimentary rocks. **Zeugens** are rare and isolated table-like masses of resistant rock left perched when the weaker underlying rock is eroded. Both landforms show fluting consistent with wind corrasion, are aligned with wind direction and occur in areas where sufficient fluvial erosion is unlikely.

Ventifacts are surface stones shaped by the abrasive action of wind. Material in suspension or saltation abrades the exposed sides of the stone, flattening and smoothing the surface. When there are three defined sides they are termed 'dreikanter' and can be used to determine past wind directions.

To sum up, the removal and transport of material by wind is an important process in shaping desert surfaces. Although the competence of wind is relatively low, it is fairly continuous and under the right conditions can dominate the landscape (as in Tibesti). However, not all deserts show extensive evidence of aeolian erosion and in all deserts water plays a role.

SECTION E

Fluvial processes

Rain in deserts?

Low rainfall is the main characteristic of deserts, but no desert is totally dry. Even extreme deserts such as the Atacama experience rain events, albeit at a low frequency. The impact of such events has led physical geographers to consider intermittent surface run-off as a major process in deserts.

Hot deserts are associated with atmospheric stability where air is descending and condensation or raindrop formation are prevented. For deserts to develop, the causes of stability must be enduring; large deserts are associated with anticyclonic systems or with major cold ocean currents (see pages 16–17). For rain to occur, these controls must be overcome and this often requires very unusual conditions.

The surfaces of deserts reach high temperatures, but the surface air cannot rise and cool to dew point because air in the upper atmosphere is descending. Weakening of the anticyclone by the invasion of a strong low-pressure system allows local air to rise, cool and condense. Such events are often associated with major and unusual movements of the tropical or mid-latitude jet streams. When surface air does rise, it contains sufficient energy to form towering clouds (cumulonimbus) and this leads to rapid condensation, giving relatively short duration but extremely intense rainfall.

Case study: El Niño

In 1999 the Atacama Desert experienced a short period of heavy rain. Atmospheric stability in this region is due to a persistent anticyclone, enhanced by an offshore cold ocean current. The rain was the outcome of a major El Niño event, causing the eastward extension of large volumes of warm surface water across the Pacific. This was sufficient to increase sea surface temperatures from the normal 14°C to over 20°C. As the coastal inversion weakened, moist maritime air was able to flow inland, bringing rain. This was the most severe El Niño event for over 100 years and it gave this region its first major rainfall for over 50 years.

Hydrological responses

Figure 2.7 The generalised desert hydrological cycle

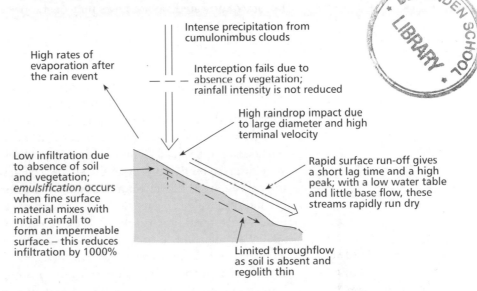

High rates of evaporation after the rain event

Intense precipitation from cumulonimbus clouds

Interception fails due to absence of vegetation; rainfall intensity is not reduced

High raindrop impact due to large diameter and high terminal velocity

Low infiltration due to absence of soil and vegetation; *emulsification* occurs when fine surface material mixes with initial rainfall to form an impermeable surface – this reduces infiltration by 1000%

Rapid surface run-off gives a short lag time and a high peak; with a low water table and little base flow, these streams rapidly run dry

Limited throughflow as soil is absent and regolith thin

The hydrological response of desert surfaces to rainfall is akin to that of an urban area with blocked drains. The normal filters of vegetation and soil are largely absent and high proportions of rainfall form surface run-off (**2.7**). Although of short duration, surface run-off often reaches a high peak discharge with high competence and capacity. This is a typical geomorphological event; an infrequent and unpredictable occurrence but capable of significant work in a short period of time. Such events are difficult (and dangerous) to study and difficult to quantify in terms of impact on the area (**2.8**).

Figure 2.8 A typical desert stream hydrograph (cusecs = cubic metres per second)

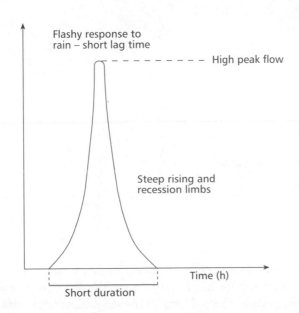

Discharge, Q (cusecs)

Flashy response to rain – short lag time

High peak flow

Steep rising and recession limbs

Time (h)

Short duration

Rivers with upper catchments in humid climates (such as, for example, the Nile and the Colorado) maintain flow through deserts. These exotic or **exogenous rivers** are often incised into deep valleys or gorges. Other channels are dry for extended periods and are referred to as **ephemeral streams**; they are a typical feature of many deserts. Deep dry ravine features or **wadis** may form large-scale and complex 'dry' drainage patterns with high drainage density (the total length of channel, wet and dry, divided by area). Once formed, such ill-defined channels persist for an extended time, as they are not infilled by mass movement or obscured by soil or vegetation. Water also moves over the surface as sheet wash. This is less efficient than channel flow but can still pick up and transport fine material. Sheet wash occurs under conditions of intense precipitation and low infiltration capacity. As the surface becomes saturated, debris flows may occur, producing delta-like features (see page 28).

Erosion

A high peak discharge gives high energy to pick up and transport load. Peak velocity determines the calibre of material that can be removed and carried by the flow (the stream's competence). In addition, there is generally much load available in deserts, as aeolian processes only remove particles of less than 0.25 mm diameter and there is an absence of vegetation to bind and protect the surface. The sediment yield of channels in arid regions is higher than in other environments. The alternating build-up and removal of surface debris is a characteristic of desert regions and over an extended time reaches an equilibrium. Desert channels also show a spatial equilibrium, as only some parts of a channel system tend to be active in a single storm event. Storms are generally fairly localised and, in combination with the rapid loss of water through evaporation and infiltration into the bed, cause the flood flow to diminish rapidly. In the Sahara, channel floodwater seldom flows for more than 300 km and is often limited to far shorter sections of the watercourse. This local discharge produces a stepping in the long profile as deposition occurs at intervals.

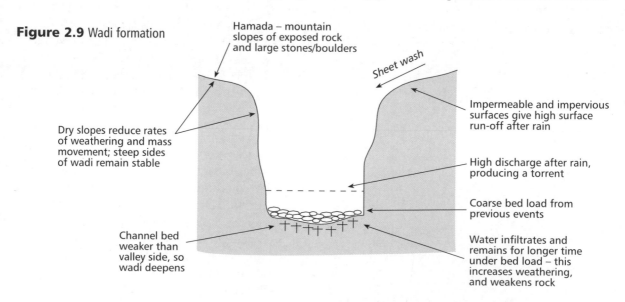

Figure 2.9 Wadi formation

Hamada – mountain slopes of exposed rock and large stones/boulders

Sheet wash

Impermeable and impervious surfaces give high surface run-off after rain

Dry slopes reduce rates of weathering and mass movement; steep sides of wadi remain stable

High discharge after rain, producing a torrent

Coarse bed load from previous events

Channel bed weaker than valley side, so wadi deepens

Water infiltrates and remains for longer time under bed load – this increases weathering, and weakens rock

Complex and extensive systems of ephemeral channels suggest that fluvial erosion was and still is significant. In addition to the direct removal of material, channels control slopes. Many of these systems are **endoreic** (flow towards a central point) or centripetal in pattern and are not controlled by a sea base-level. Wadis or gulches (USA) provide comprehensive evidence for fluvial erosion in both pattern and form. These deep and steep-sided ravines do not show alignment to the prevailing wind but tend towards fluvial dendritic patterns. Wadi floors are littered with coarse material (bed load) that shows evidence of rounding through corrasion and attrition (**2.9**). On gentler slopes, channels often show braiding, characterised by wide, poorly defined beds choked with stones, cobbles and sand.

Alluvial fans are cone-like accumulations of deposited material that form where ephemeral streams emerge from uplands and the velocity of the floodwater falls. The fans may coalesce to form a more continuous slope called a **bahada**. These features show typical fluvial sorting by particle size over distance (large to small) and a vertical stratification (representing events of different magnitude). The layers of fans may also include clays and silts that have moved down the valley as mudflows.

Many rivers in desert regions terminate in inland basins. Following rain events, these basins become temporary stores in the form of shallow lakes. Clays and silts transported by the ephemeral streams as load are deposited and, after evaporation, salts carried in solution are also deposited. These features are termed playas and can form extensive plains (Lake Eyre in Australia reaches 9300 km^2). When dry, the surface consists of fine clays and silts or salts (**evaporites**) that often show polygonal patterning from desiccation and shrinking. The playa floor aggrades as new material is added, but fine material is removed through deflation so that this 'depositional' landform can develop to below sea level.

That completes an examination of the main processes at work in hot desert environments. The next chapter looks at the outcomes of those processes.

Review

14 Try to explain why it can sometimes rain in desert areas.

15 How does the absence of vegetation affect the hydrological cycle in desert regions?

16 Why do desert streams have a high competence and capacity after rainstorms?

Enquiry

1 With reference to a hot desert region or area that you have studied in detail:
   a attempt to discover the past climate(s) of the region and the impact that these had on the present landscape
   b identify and discuss evidence for fluvial erosion and fluvial deposition.

2 Why are rates of denudation relatively low in your chosen area?

3

Hot desert environments

In this chapter, the discussion of hot desert environments continues. Attention focuses on three particular outcomes of the processes and conditions examined in the previous chapter. They are landforms, soils and ecosystems.

Landforms

Slopes

All landforms may be seen as particular arrangements of different slope elements. Desert slopes are distinctive in character as they are exposed, are often angular and can be divided into segments (**3.1**). As with other desert landforms, there is considerable controversy surrounding the origin of these systems. There are typically four slope components: mountain front, pediment, bahada and playa.

Figure 3.1 A piedmont slope system

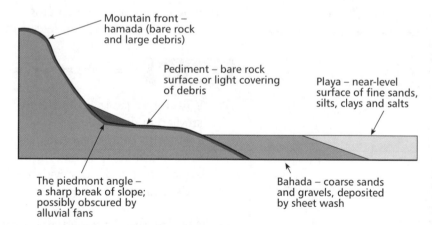

Mountain front – hamada (bare rock and large debris)

Pediment – bare rock surface or light covering of debris

Playa – near-level surface of fine sands, silts, clays and salts

The piedmont angle – a sharp break of slope; possibly obscured by alluvial fans

Bahada – coarse sands and gravels, deposited by sheet wash

Upland areas typically have steep slopes and are incised by deep valleys, ravines or canyons. The low rainfall limits slope reduction through weathering and mass movement. Mountain fronts are characterised by tracts of exposed rock and large-calibre debris (known as **hamada**; see **3.1**). In Arizona, old peneplain surfaces have been breached by fluvial and aeolian processes to leave isolated flat-topped pillars (**buttes**) or tables (**mesas**). In areas of igneous rock, variations in the frequency of jointing cause differential mechanical and chemical weathering, producing dramatic outcrops of resistant bedrock, which are called **inselbergs**.

Pediments are a characteristic feature of deserts. They are regular slopes of between 5 and 10° at the base of the mountain front (**3.1**). This is similar to a scree slope (talus) as the surface is littered with coarse debris. However, the debris is only a veneer over a regular bedrock surface and the slope has not developed through accumulation. Rather, the pediment is a slope of transport in a state of dynamic equilibrium, as the input of debris from the mountain front balances the output through sheet wash. The **bahada** is a slope with a generally slightly lower angle than the pediment and the two often merge into a single slightly concave surface. Unlike the pediment, the bahada is an aggradational slope and consists of coarse sands and gravel deposited by sheet wash off the mountain front and pediment. This may show some bedding that marks distinct rain events. Finally, there is the **playa**, a near-level surface formed from the fine clays, silts and sands washed into the depression, as well as from evaporate.

Desert slopes are distinctive because of the unusual combination and frequency of processes. In general, relief is severe and this reflects the weak presence of mass movement. Variations in rock resistance (structure and lithology) tend to be emphasised, as the denudational processes are generally weak. Where effective erosion does occur it tends to be localised, adding to the severity of relief.

Sand features

The stereotypical desert landscape of a 'sea of sand' (**3.2**) is less common than mountainous terrain. Dune landscapes only comprise of 0.6 per cent of desert areas in the south-west of the USA, and only rise to 12 per cent in the Sahara and over 30 per cent in Australia. The Rub-al-Khali in Saudi Arabia covers $570\,000$ km^2 as a continuous sand sea and it is estimated that 99.8 per cent of sand in deserts is found in **ergs** (sand sheets) of over 125 km^2.

Figure 3.2 The Grand Erg Occidental (the Sahara)

Type of dune	Morphology	Sand supply	Wind characteristics	Veget- ation	Movement	Example locations
Barchan	Crescent-shaped individual dunes. The horns of the crescent point down wind. Dunes may reach 200 m in height. These dunes are rare and represent 0.01% of desert sand!	Limited. Dunes are generally surrounded by a bare desert surface.	A prevailing wind with less than 20° deviation. The direction is at right angles to the dune.	None.	Highly mobile and often invade an adjacent semi-arid area. Problem for communications and agriculture. Speeds of 50 metres a year have been recorded.	The Atacama Desert, Peru; Egypt.
Akle dune (also termed barchanoid ridges)	Coalescing crescent-shaped barchans forming a series of ridges at right angles to the prevailing wind. Sometimes called a fish-scale dune pattern.	Slightly greater sand availability than barchans. Some patches of exposed surface between ridges.	Constant prevailing wind but significant local turbulence caused by the ridges.	None.	Less mobile than barchans, as greater quantities of sand are involved.	Egypt.
Seif dunes	Long sinuous dunes, extending for over 100 km and reaching 200 m in height. The ridges often show low and regular summits. The ridges often run parallel to each other, up to 10 km apart.	Large quantities of sand available and little exposed rock present.	Thought to be produced by crosswinds. One wind is prevailing (Trades), while the secondary wind may be diurnal or seasonal. These funnel the sand into a ridge.	None.	Some movement along the dune. The windward end is generally blunt and the leeward is tapered. Little movement of the main dune.	Egypt, southern Iran and Libya. Seifs require large flat areas.
Pyramid dunes or star dunes (rhourds)	Steep radiating slopes from one or several peaks. These can reach 300 m in height and extend to 2 km at their base.	Moderate sand availability. These often occur in conjunction with other dunes and there is little exposed rock surface.	Wind from a number of directions, with no dominant prevailing wind direction.	None.	Virtually no movement, as the dune is being shaped from all sides.	Namibia.

Figure 3.3 Dune types

Sand refers to a particle size (between 0.95 and 2.0 mm in diameter). It is largely composed of quartz that is resistant to chemical weathering and hard enough to resist fracture during movement. However, sand also contains mica, feldspar and other rock fragments, and may vary in colour from white, through yellow and brown to black. The concentration of sands in deserts is the result of a long and complex history involving past as well as present climates and processes. Sand is initially formed by weathering and through abrasion or corrasion. In humid climates, large proportions of sand are incorporated into the soil and it is only in coastal areas that pure sand accumulates. In deserts, soil formation is extremely limited and the finer clays and silts are removed by aeolian erosion. Sand is too large to be removed in suspension and accumulates at the surface. It is also thought that fluvial processes during the wetter climates of the Quaternary period deposited much of the sand in present deserts.

Dunes are dynamic landforms that reflect a balance between erosion, transport and deposition. Their mobility and changes in morphology provide fascinating material for geomorphologists. Wind direction and speed largely determine the morphology of dunes, but local factors including load availability, relief, the texture of the sand and surface obstructions may also be important (**3.3**). Dunes are often asymmetrical, with a gentle slope on the windward side and a steeper slope to the lee (**3.4**). As a dune develops, it modifies the wind at the surface through turbulence. To the lee of dunes the slip face may cause the local wind direction to reverse, causing localised erosion and a steepening of the slope. Wind may also be funnelled between dunes, increasing wind speed, and certain dune formations can cause helical flows.

Figure 3.4 Barkhan development

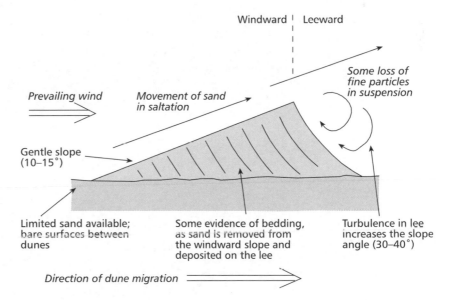

Windward | Leeward

Prevailing wind   Movement of sand in saltation

Some loss of fine particles in suspension

Gentle slope (10–15°)

Limited sand available; bare surfaces between dunes

Some evidence of bedding, as sand is removed from the windward slope and deposited on the lee

Turbulence in lee increases the slope angle (30–40°)

Direction of dune migration

Case study: The Atacama Desert, Arequipa (southern Peru)

The Atacama has an average rainfall of less than 10 mm a year. Restricted to a narrow coastal strip, it does not contain large sand seas and local relief frequently modifies the prevailing SSW wind. The sand supply is from weathered sedimentary rocks and from dry river beds and old lake floors. With limited sand supply, barchan dune fields are the main features, although transverse dunes and tied dunes occur when local relief disrupts movement. In the area shown in **3.5**, the barchans are poorly developed, with an average height of 1–2 m, a shallow windward slope at 4.2° and a steeper lee slope of 28°. The distance between the horns is only 25 m, whereas on a larger plain area 10 km away, barchans develop over a greater distance and are significantly larger, reaching a height of 3–4 m, slopes of 11° and 39°, and a width of 34 m. Where the movement of individual barchans is slowed by relief, the dunes coalesce to form a transverse dune (similar to an akle) and to the lee of the obstruction the sand is aligned into a tied dune running parallel to the prevailing wind.

Figure 3.5 A field sketch of a dune system near Arequipa (Peru)

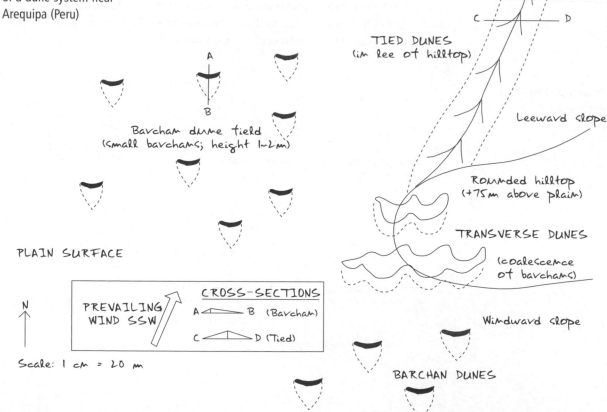

1 Attempt to explain why desert slopes are often angular in form.

2 Describe the difference between **pediment** and **bahada** slopes.

3 Outline the processes that deposit and erode material in a playa.

4 Identify the potential sources of the sand in dune systems.

5 Why do dunes show such a variety of shapes?

6 Attempt to explain why some dunes are 'fixed' while others are 'mobile'.

SECTION B

The past and the present

In geomorphological terms, many of the present desert areas are relatively inert. The rates of weathering, mass movement, erosion and deposition are significantly less than in other environments. This slow rate increases the significance of past climates and past processes. During the Quaternary period (from approximately 20 million to 10 000 years ago) there was a significant cooling of global temperatures, producing a very different pattern of climate. Essentially, the climatic zones moved towards the Equator. It is difficult to reconstruct the precise climates of the Quaternary, but we do know that present deserts were considerably more humid and that there was extensive vegetation and fauna. Under this near-temperate climate, more active weathering, mass movement and fluvial processes would have occurred, and it is these landscapes that are still evident in today's deserts.

In desert areas there is considerable evidence that climate and processes in the past were very different to those found today (**3.6**).

The role of past climate is generally seen as shaping the background for current processes. The major depressions and extensive plains could have been formed by fluvial erosion (**peneplanation**) and rivers could also have eroded the flat areas between present-day buttes and mesas in Arizona. Fluvial deposition can explain the availability of sand for dune formation and a more humid past can account for inselberg formation. In these respects, current desert processes are modifying a pre-existing landscape rather than creating a new one. The exact balance between past and present is difficult to determine and may well vary in different deserts. What is clear is that the past is significant in virtually all deserts and must be considered when attempting to understand the present. Modern approaches to desert geomorphology see both wind and water operating in a complex and changing pattern over extended time. At its simplest, this approach proposes that the macro-landscape relates to past climates, while present-day processes of wind and water are rearranging surface material and making minor modifications.

Figure 3.6 Evidence of climatic change

Archaeological evidence

- In the Central Sahara, an ancient civilisation (the Garamantes) was pastoral and left cave paintings of temperate animals and activities.
- From Roman records we know that significant quantities of grain were produced in areas of North Africa that are now desert.
- The Atacama Desert once supported a flourishing civilisation based on agriculture. Remains of cities and terraced fields attest to their scale and prosperity.
- Pollen grains from oak and cedar have been found in the Central Sahara, as have remains of small crocodiles.
- Extensive semi-fossilised forests (mainly stumps and trunks) have been found in the Sahara.

Geomorphological evidence

- Lake Chad in the south-central Sahara was once 30 000 km^2 in extent, 120 m deeper than at present and water from the lake flowed southwards into the Atlantic Ocean. Such a large-scale river could only be supported by a significantly higher rainfall.
- Satellite images taken over Egypt show extensive river channels cut into the bedrock but now obscured by 5 m of sand.
- Throughout the Sahara, there is evidence that river systems were once far larger and more persistent than today. Such systems could only develop under conditions of higher rainfall.

Review

7 Why are past, or relict, landforms still so evident in desert landscapes?

8 How has satellite imagery helped in discovering past landscapes?

9 What are the likely future implications for deserts of global warming?

SECTION C

Soils, flora and fauna

Soils

The two main ingredients of soils, inorganic and organic material, are both scarce in arid environments. Regolith is shallow and the sparse vegetation does not contribute a regular supply of dead organic material. In addition, the scarcity of water and dead organic material inhibits micro-organism activity and there is little sorting of surface material. Little detailed research has been carried out on arid soils. They tend to be azonal in character, with a colour, mineral content and horizons that reflect parent material rather than soil-forming processes. Frequently, the surface layer identified as 'soil' is little more than regolith with few signs of sorting. However, within arid zones more complex soils do occur, although generally these seem to be products of past and more humid climates.

With an annual water balance of precipitation less than the potential evaporation, the dominant movement of water is upwards. Groundwater is drawn towards the surface by capillary action and this leads to an increase in the concentration of salt in the upper horizons. This process is termed **salinisation** and leads to the formation of **solonchak** soils (when bases accumulate in the upper horizons but pH does not exceed 8) and **solonetz** soils (when a hard highly alkaline layer forms just beneath the surface). These soils are alkaline and are generally termed **pedocals**.

Flora

The scarcity of water and alkalinity produce a hostile environment for plants, fauna and people. In order to survive, specialisation is necessary. Lack of water is the main barrier, as deserts have a high potential for photosynthesis. The rate of nutrient cycling is extremely low, with an average **net primary productivity** (NPP) of less than 0.003 kilos per square metre a year (this can be compared with 2.2 in tropical rain forests and 1.3 for evergreen temperate forests).

Figure **3.7** is a systems diagram illustrating the **flow** of energy between **stores** in a desert environment. The flows are low and the stores relatively small. There are other noteworthy features:

- Although relatively unstructured, the soil is the largest store. Dead organic matter returning from fauna and plants, litter is slow to decompose and becomes trapped in the soil. Leaching is minimal, reducing the loss of nutrients. Soil nutrients also include 'dry' minerals that are unavailable to plants.
- The soil nutrients are available after rain to support rapid vegetation growth. This also gives the soil some potential on irrigation.
- The small size of the biomass store (B) reflects both sparseness and the lack of vertical development.
- The large flow from biomass to litter (L) represents the shedding of leaves and stems by plants during periods of water deficit. Many plants wither and die back during extended dry periods.
- The litter store is small, as dead organic matter is consumed by insects or removed from the surface by wind or water.

Plants are adapted to desert environments in five main ways:

- Deep root systems allow plants to exploit groundwater to considerable depths. Plants invest energy in deep tap roots, rather than in productive foliage. The above ground to below ground ratio may be as high as 1 : 25. Such plants are termed **phreatophytes**. Competition

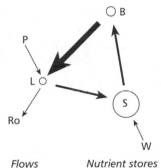

Flows

P Precipitation
Ro Run-off
W Weathering

Nutrient stores

L Litter
B Biomass
S Soil

Figure 3.7 The desert nutrient cycle: flows and stores are shown proportionally

between plants on the surface is low, so that vertical development and canopies are not required.

- Leaves and stems are generally specialised to reduce water loss through transpiration. Stomata are infrequent and can close when rates of water loss are too high, and are also located on the underside of leaves in shade. The leaves are waxy and thick, decreasing the surface area to mass ratio and allowing water to be stored away from the leaf surface. This group of plants is termed **xerophytes**.
- Many plants have developed complex water storage systems in leaves, stems and trunks so that water can be absorbed during spells of rain surplus. This group of plants includes cacti and the baobab tree.
- Many smaller plants, including flowers, have developed seeds that can withstand extended periods of dormancy. Germination is triggered by rain and the plant shoots flowers and reproduces within a few weeks before dying back as the water is evaporated. Such plants may reproduce infrequently but can transform deserts such as the Atacama into a sea of flowers after rain.
- Leaves and stems are often protected by alkaline toxins or by thorns. In a desert environment, potential food for animals is scarce, so that plants that can survive are under considerable pressure from herbivores. Cacti are one of the most protected of plants and are resistant to most pests.

It is difficult to generalise about desert vegetation as it varies considerably over both time and place. Salt pans (**playas**) are generally bare of vegetation, as the accumulation of salts, at over 7 per cent, is too hostile. The slopes immediately around playas, other low-salinity depressions and the channels of ephemeral streams are colonised by phreatophytes. These species can tap the groundwater beneath the surface and tend to grow in zones depending on the level of salinisation. In the USA, pickleweed grows nearest the salt pan, as it can tolerate up to 6 per cent salt content in groundwater, followed by arrow-weed (< 3 per cent) and finally honey mesquite, that can tolerate salt levels up to 0.5 per cent.

On slopes away from depressions, particularly on the bahada gravels, groundwater is too deep and xerophytes colonise. The roots of these plants do not extend to the water table and require aeration, as well as being intolerant to salt levels above 0.25 per cent. Where salinity is higher on the bahada, plants such as the creosote bush give way to desert holly. Although sparse, vegetation is not randomly distributed, but responds to local changes in the quality and quantity of groundwater. The level of salinity appears to be particularly important, reinforcing the idea that plants are competing against the environment rather than against each other.

Fauna

Animal and insect life is highly dependent on the level of primary production. Plants synthesise complex organic material from carbon dioxide, nutrients, water and sunlight through the process of photosynthesis. This provides food for higher trophic levels. The carrying capacity of arid areas is limited by the food supply, particularly as many plants are well protected. Herbivores are relatively uncommon and a large proportion of the goats, sheep, horses and camels have not evolved in arid environments but have 'invaded'. Insects and reptiles tend to dominate and appear to have evolved in desert environments. The fauna is adapted to this environment in a number of ways:

- Much of the fauna lives below the surface. Few breeding habitats on the surface offer protection and beneath the surface temperature is moderated.
- Animals have evolved unusual renal systems so that urine is highly concentrated, reducing the rate of water loss. Camels have further developed water storage systems, allowing prolonged time and activity without renewing water supplies.
- Many animals are nocturnal, gathering food and reproducing during the night when temperatures are significantly lower and water loss is reduced.
- Insects generally have hard and waterproof skins to prevent surface loss of water and to reduce the threat from predators. Many, such as the scorpion, are aggressive and possess the capability effectively to defend themselves against larger predators and to attack prey.
- Much of the fauna consists of scavengers or organisms that are able to exploit a wide range of food supplies (**omnivores**). Dead animals and dead plants provide a productive source of food and this is fully exploited by insects and reptiles.
- Desert fringes are also visited by migrating species (such as, for example, the locust), particularly in seasons associated with periodic rains.
- The highest trophic level, the large carnivores, is poorly represented in desert environments, as dependency on meat would require too large an area to find sufficient prey.

Deserts are hostile and fragile environments. The combination of heat and aridity means that fauna and flora survive, but seldom dominate, and the occurrence of 'events' can produce radical and rapid change. Deserts have provided a severe challenge for man, as the large areas of under-utilised and sparsely populated land have acted as magnets in an increasingly crowded world. The question of how these areas can be exploited in a sustainable manner will be examined in **Chapter 5**.

Review

10 Describe some of the ways in which plants adapt to a desert environment.

11 What is meant by the term **net primary productivity** (NPP)?

12 Why is the NPP of desert vegetation so low?

1   Select one image of a desert landscape from any source (Internet, textbook, journal and so on).
    a   Construct an annotated sketch diagram to show the main features.
    b   Select two features and, for each, write an explanatory account of their formation.
    c   Identify and explain likely processes of weathering and mass movement at work in the area of your image.

2   Construct a simple systems diagram to show the inputs and outputs for a sand dune system. Attempt to include the potential sources of the sand as well as to where it is removed.
    a   Identify the type of system that you have drawn. Justify your answer.
    b   How could a systems approach help in the management of sand dune systems?

4

Semi-arid environments

Climate

Semi-arid environments (BS in the Köppen classification) form a transition zone between desert and humid landscapes. They have an annual water deficit but there is sufficient seasonal rain to affect processes, vegetation and land use. A typical feature is the unreliability of seasonal rain. Rainfall frequently falls significantly below average levels, causing drought. This should not be confused with aridity, as it is concerned with water balance rather than with total amounts (see page 14). The failure of rain has severe repercussions for people, as well as an important role in determining vegetation, soil and landform development.

Semi-arid regions lie between the ascending and descending branches of the Hadley cell (**1.6**). Rains occur when the ascending branch dominates, and dry seasons with the descending branch. The movement of the Earth in relation to the Sun is regular, but the movement of the Hadley and Ferrel cells is not quite so reliable. The balancing of these global pressure systems is not fully understood, but variations in solar radiation and changes in the jet streams – as well as surface events such as El Niño – are thought to affect the global circulation.

Case study: The north-east of Brazil (the Sertão)

North-east Brazil lies well within the Tropics and has a mean annual rainfall of nearly 800 mm. Between July and December the average monthly rainfall is less than 10 mm and over half the total rain falls in March and April. The defined dry season is accompanied by average temperatures above 28°C, causing a severe water deficit. However, in some years the rains fail almost totally, while in others the rains are considerably greater than average. This, then, is a region of both drought and flood. The main reason for this is that the north-east of Brazil projects eastwards into the equatorial maritime high-pressure system, located over the Atlantic. When this high strengthens in July (winter), the north-east remains dry under anticyclonic conditions. In January, the weakening of the Atlantic high allows the intertropical convergence zone (ITCZ) to extend southwards over the interior of Brazil. The ITCZ introduces tropical maritime air from the Atlantic, which is both moist and unstable and brings rain. When the ITCZ unpredictably fails to move sufficiently south, the north-east remains under the influence of the Atlantic high and the rains fail.

Similar problems with rainfall reliability occur in other areas where seasonal rain is determined by a fine balance between the ITCZ and high-pressure systems. The Sahel in Africa has an unreliable rainy season that periodically causes severe droughts, as do Australia and the interior of China.

Review

1 Distinguish between the terms **drought** and **aridity**.

2 Why is rainfall in semi-arid regions often unreliable but heavy when it does occur?

Processes

Weathering and mass movement

With a greater supply of water and with high temperatures, the rate of chemical weathering increases sufficiently for a layer of regolith to form over much of the surface. In addition, rates of mechanical weathering through salt crystal growth and wetting and drying further break up the surface rock. Biological weathering becomes significant as plants extend deep roots into cracks in the rock to obtain supplies of deep groundwater.

Figure 4.1 Gully formation in a (humid) semi-arid environment

With greater rates of weathering and with higher rainfall for lubrication, mass movement is more vigorous than in desert areas. The seasonal rain is sufficient to saturate the surface and increase the stress force, while cohesion is reduced and the discontinuous vegetation does not provide effective protection. The greater frequency of mass movement reduces the steepness of slopes and debris accumulating at the base of slopes produces convex/concave slopes (**4.1**). These landscapes are probably also influenced by past fluvial environments during the Quaternary period.

Erosion

The effectiveness of aeolian processes is greatly reduced by the (albeit discontinuous) vegetation cover. The scrub, shrub and tree vegetation reduces the surface wind speed by increasing turbulence and the vegetation provides some physical binding of the surface, reducing the rate of drying so that surface particles are heavier. Where vegetation has been removed aeolian processes become dominant, with the formation of deflation hollows and even localised dunes. This process may become progressive and plays an important role in **desertification** (see page 52).

The sediment yields of rivers in semi-arid regions are among the highest of all rivers, attesting to the importance of fluvial erosion. High-intensity fluvial processes occur in areas of water deficit because semi-arid environments provide high-velocity surface run-off and a high load availability.

Semi-arid areas heat rapidly during the summer (see the data for Timbuktu, **1.5**) causing extensive loss of surface water. The rains may be limited in duration but they are intense in character and often exceed the infiltration capacity of the surface, producing a high proportion of surface run-off. Vegetation is generally too discontinuous to provide an effective barrier through interception and the soil is not deep enough to infiltrate and hold the deluge. Vegetation partially protects the surface against raindrop impact and sheet wash but, without a surface root mat, the soil has low resistance and is rapidly eroded and transported into channels. Where the natural vegetation has been disturbed, erosion accelerates.

Review

3 Compare semi-arid and arid environments in terms of:

- weathering processes

- mass movement

- erosion processes.

4 Attempt to explain why semi-arid areas have high levels of fluvial erosion despite a low total rainfall.

Landforms

Semi-arid environments tend to be more distinctive in terms of vegetation and land use than in terms of landforms. However, the features of gullies and braided channels stand out in semi-arid environments, although they are not unique to these conditions.

Gullies are steep-sided ephemeral channels that are generally cut into relatively weak material and that run as networks directly down slopes (**4.1**). Gullies are often recently formed features and can give extremely high drainage densities (in the Badlands of South Dakota on clay, the drainage density can reach over 1300, in comparison with densities of between two and ten in the UK). Gullies develop on slopes where vegetation has been disturbed. The high peak discharge rapidly cuts deep channels that then collect further precipitation. Such systems are capable of eroding large quantities of soil and regolith, and are almost always considered as undesirable.

Braided channels are characterised by extreme width and shallowness in cross-section and by a complex series of diverging and converging channels, separated by banks and bars, in plan (**4.2**). Braiding is associated with extreme seasonal variations in discharge, high load availability and sparse vegetation. With intense rain and low capacities of interception and infiltration, rivers in semi-arid regions show a flashy response with a short lag time. The greater frequency of high discharge in semi-arid areas produces a more clearly defined channel and features that continue downstream, while in arid regions these tend to peter out quickly. The rapid change in stream velocity results in bed load being picked up and transported, only to be deposited as velocity decreases. This causes choking of the channel, with the deposition of sands and gravel to form banks and

Figure 4.2 The main characteristics of a braided channel

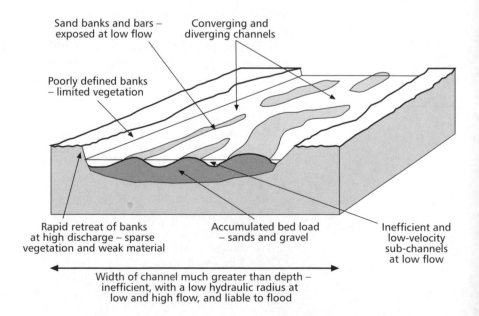

Sand banks and bars – exposed at low flow

Converging and diverging channels

Poorly defined banks – limited vegetation

Rapid retreat of banks at high discharge – sparse vegetation and weak material

Accumulated bed load – sands and gravel

Inefficient and low-velocity sub-channels at low flow

Width of channel much greater than depth – inefficient, with a low hydraulic radius at low and high flow, and liable to flood bars on the bed. The high discharge also causes accelerated bank erosion that releases more material into the river, contributing further to the bed load. Widening of the channel occurs because the valley floor is only partially protected by vegetation. Such rivers are often ephemeral and will nearly dry up during extended dry spells or droughts. During these inactive phases the channel bed is colonised by vegetation, which is swept away in subsequent floods. Gullying on the steeper slopes of the upper catchments tends to increase braiding downstream as load is added.

Review

5 Explain why drainage densities are often high in semi-arid regions.

6 What are the factors that tend to cause river channels to braid?

7 Why do semi-arid regions often contain relief features that formed under previous climatic conditions?

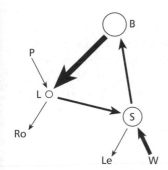

Flows
P Precipitation
Ro Run-off
Le Leaching
W Weathering

Nutrient stores
L Litter
B Biomass
S Soil

Figure 4.3 The semi-arid (thorn–scrub) nutrient cycle: flows and stores are shown proportionally

Soils and ecosystems

Soils in semi-arid areas are alkaline, shallow and lacking in clear horizons, and are referred to as **chestnut-brown**. The accumulation of organic matter in the top 25 cm is sufficient to colour the topsoil and to increase water retention. This soil develops under discontinuous vegetation cover and supports a significant fauna. Salts concentrate in the upper horizons, often forming nodules, as precipitation is less than evaporation.

The following features of the semi-arid nutrient cycle need to be emphasised (**4.3**):

- The largest nutrient store in the semi-arid nutrient cycle is in the biomass, as there is sufficient seasonal water to allow vertical growth with thin trunks and branches.
- At intervals, fire releases the nutrients from the biomass to circulate rapidly through the litter and into the soil to promote vegetation growth.
- Litter decomposes fairly rapidly through micro-organisms (in particular, ants and termites).
- Micro-organisms and periodic rain return nutrients to the soil fairly rapidly, although loss through leaching becomes significant.
- The loss of nutrients by sheet wash is balanced by more rapid rates of weathering.
- In general, the stores and the nutrient flows are significantly larger than those of desert systems.

Case study: The caatinga of north-east Brazil

The interior of the north-east of Brazil has a seasonal and unreliable rainfall (see Quixeramobim, 1.5) and the Precambrian rocks weather slowly to form patchy, coarse and sandy soils separated by areas of exposed rock. Water availability varies greatly with geology and slope, producing some areas of richer vegetation.

The vegetation is largely thorn scrub with patches of coarse tussock grass and isolated stands of palm trees. Xerophytic species such as cacti dominate in the drier areas, while palms, 'bottle' trees and shrubs colonise the moister areas (4.4). The thorny scrub remains dry and leafless for much of the year and forms a dense tangle of stems with a thin dry litter. The vegetation is protected from herbivores by thorns and the leaves, produced after rain, are prickly and hard. The scrub plants have deep root systems, but for much of the year are virtually dormant due to the water shortage. Rain triggers rapid growth and many of the plants go through rapid reproductive cycles. Insect life dominates, although rodents are also common. The palm species provide valuable food and resources for both fauna and local populations, and it is these that sustain life in the caatinga.

Figure 4.4 A baobab tree

In semi-arid environments, the flora and fauna are in competition with the climatic environment as much as with other species. Most organisms are specialised for specific niches and the nutrient cycles and food webs are finely balanced. Such systems are inherently fragile, as any interference in the natural environment tends to cause rapid degradation. The sustainable exploitation of these areas has always been demanding, but in recent decades, with increasing pressure for land, it has become an urgent issue.

Review

8 How do the nutrient stores and flows differ between semi-arid and arid ecosystems?

9 Why is semi-arid vegetation often thorny?

10 Why are the trophic levels in semi-arid areas more complex than in arid areas?

1   Construct a systems diagram to show why gullying should increase after the reduction of vegetation in a semi-arid environment. Include details of the local hydrological cycle and fluvial processes.

2   Research one example of a major drought in a semi-arid region that you have studied.
    a   Attempt to explain why the rains failed in your chosen example.
    b   What was the impact of the drought on the flora and fauna of the area?
    c   To what extent can your example be seen as having human rather than physical causes?

People and the dry Tropics

The survival of indigenous people

Deserts are associated with sparse populations, but they have also been inhabited by large and relatively sophisticated civilisations. For example, the Bushmen (or San) of the Kalahari have survived in extremely arid conditions for at least 9000 years, and have done so without degrading their environment. Traditionally, they were labelled as 'hunter–gatherers'. However, it has recently become apparent that this group had a significant agricultural base. They also domesticated animals. What has also become clear is that they did not evolve in their present arid environment, but were driven off more humid and productive land by larger and more competitive tribal and colonising groups. By 1980, only 5 per cent of the remaining 50 000 San people relied for their existence on hunting–gathering activities. Similarly, it is thought that the Aborigines of Australia were pushed on to increasingly arid land by colonists and lost access to agricultural land that had formerly supplemented their hunting–gathering activities. By 1980, the majority of the remaining 160 000 Aborigines were not following a traditional lifestyle. In recent years, however, there has been something of a return to the old lifestyle (**5.1**).

Figure 5.1 Modern Aboriginal ritual

The key to desert survival has, in part, been in living in small, isolated communities. It is estimated that, per person, Bushmen require 7 km^2 of space, while the Aborigines need almost 80 km^2. Survival also depends on an efficient seasonal cycle that fully exploits all of the available resources. Desert dwellers tend to be omnivorous, with over 50 per cent of available plant and animal species eaten regularly. In addition, such groups often possess a knowledge of water resources and ecological patterns that goes beyond the capabilities of Western science. With few material possessions, they are mobile and able to adapt rapidly to changing conditions. There is little evidence that starvation has ever been a major cause of death. Indeed, the whole life-support system emerges as being extremely efficient. It has been calculated that two-thirds of a group could provide food for the entire group in only one-third of the available time, implying that potential leisure time may well be in excess of that in current Western cultures. In coastal desert areas, the sea forms a valuable supply of food, and the recent discovery of mummified bodies in the sand dunes of Chile, near Arica, is evidence of a flourishing Chinchorro culture, dated to around 9000 BC.

The nomadic exploitation of plant and animal resources by a low-density population appears to have had only a limited effect on natural ecosystems. Fire was used extensively as a tool in hunting and, possibly, to induce pasture growth after rains. Controlled fires are an effective method of driving game towards waiting hunters, and such fires would have been left to burn. It is possible that these strategies had an impact in semi-arid areas where woodland would not regenerate. It has also been suggested that hunting led to the decline of large game in semi-arid areas, and that this in turn forced populations to turn to agriculture.

SECTION B

Irrigation

The key to sustaining larger populations in the dry Tropics lies in increasing food supply. The most obvious way to do this is to try to raise agricultural productivity. Achieving this largely requires overcoming water deficits by means of irrigation.

Quite large ancient desert civilisations have existed and have done so mainly through the development of irrigation. This allowed the agricultural potential of high solar radiation to be exploited and to provide sufficient food to support a denser and often urban population. Irrigation probably represents the earliest attempt by people to control and modify the natural environment. It appears to have developed independently in China, the Middle East (in Iran, it is dated at *circa* 5500 BC) and the Americas. The extent of environmental modification can be illustrated by the lower Nile, which is estimated to provide the equivalent of 2983 mm rainfall in a region that receives only 127 mm. Irrigation is central to colonising desert areas and although, by 1980, only 3.7 per cent of arid lands were irrigated, these supported the bulk of the population.

Irrigation involves the artificial supply of water to an area in order to make up a water deficit and to allow the cultivation of crops. Irrigation appears to be a straightforward solution, but in practice it is both difficult and potentially degrading to the environment, and has become a major cause of abandoned land. Water can be gained from two main sources:

- **Surface water** – bringing in water, often by canal, from regions of water surplus or from adjacent exotic rivers. The energy to move such water is provided by gravity. Such water is derived from either precipitation or rivers. Water from the latter is relatively neutral and contains some nutrients.
- **Groundwater** – abstracting water from layers of rock beneath the surface. Aquifers are not unusual in desert regions, but the water contained therein has infiltrated through the surface, gaining a high load in solution, and tends to be alkaline. Energy is required to lift the water to the surface.

The earliest irrigation schemes used river diversion techniques with low technology. The silt carried by a river was deposited on flooded fields, thereby renewing fertility. Such gravity schemes led to the early settlement of desert areas in Peru, along the Nile and in China. They created some of the earliest man-made landscapes. Referred to as **hydraulic landscapes (5.2)**, these contained urban settlements, continuous fields, routes and canals. The modification of the natural environment also allowed the introduction of exotic plant species which, in turn, gave yields many times higher than native rain-fed crops. In areas without access to gravity flows of water, the more laborious technique of groundwater abstraction was used. This produced less water at a higher cost, and had a less dramatic impact on food supply and population.

Modern techniques in irrigation were mainly developed in North America. Initially, they were private ventures, but they eventually culminated in a major scheme to divert water from the Colorado River, through Mexico and into southern California. This required a diversion canal over 90 km long,

Figure 5.2 An early man-made landscape of irrigated terraces (now abandoned)

and marked the point at which schemes became too costly and complex for private enterprise. From the 1930s onwards, Federally funded schemes, often associated with major dams and hydroelectric schemes, became dominant: these included the Californian Aqueduct, that transfers water from the north to the south of California. The use of diverted water has also changed from predominantly agricultural to urban domestic and industrial consumption. Since 1960, there has been a return to private irrigation ventures, with the abstraction of local groundwater for boom and sprinkler irrigation.

In the short term, irrigation radically changes the flora and fauna. Quite simply, the desert ceases to be deserted and the natural vegetation is rapidly displaced by new species. The area of arid lands decreases and natural environments are lost. Central Valley in California is now an important agricultural region, but before 1800 it was a playa with associated bahadas and pediment zones. In the longer term, the problem with irrigation is **salinisation**, which causes soil degradation. Rain water is 'distilled', but river water and groundwater contain bases in solution. High rates of evaporation from the surface lift groundwater upward by capillary action and the bases are precipitated in the upper soil. The progressive increase in alkalinity is an inherent problem of irrigation and can often lead to soil infertility within 20 years. This is a major global problem, with an estimated 8.5 million km^2 affected in arid and semi-arid regions by 1980. To prevent the build-up of salt, drainage of the water used in irrigation is necessary and this greatly adds to the cost.

Irrigation also affects the source areas. In diversion schemes, the discharge of the host river is radically affected: by the mid-1960s, the Colorado was barely reaching the sea. The deep reservoirs accumulate cold water, radically changing the habitat for fish and plants downstream (a particular problem on the Colorado). Groundwater abstraction can severely lower the water table. One ranch in Texas lowered the water table from 12 m to 30 m below the surface between 1949 and 1968. Water tables may be lowered over significant areas, with surrounding phreatophytes replaced by xerophytic species.

Case study: California – is irrigation sustainable?

Irrigation has been practised in California for over 150 years. The water deficit has been reduced by both groundwater abstraction (67 billion litre–days) and by surface supplies along the Californian Aqueduct (**5.3**) with serious environmental side-effects. In the San Joaquin Valley, local areas subsided by as much as 8.9 m between 1928 and 1975, even causing a sag to develop in the middle of the Californian Aqueduct. Moving water south to Los Angeles is expensive, as it has to be pumped over mountain ranges. This pumping is the largest user of electricity in California, consuming sufficient power for a major city. The surface-transferred water is heavily subsidised by Federal funds, so that users pay only 10 per cent of the true costs. This has encouraged the retention of 'flooding' irrigation that uses 30 per cent more water than sprinklers, although it has a lower capital cost. To meet an ever larger demand, California has started to look at source regions even further to the humid north, in Oregon and even Canada.

Figure 5.3 The Californian water diversion scheme

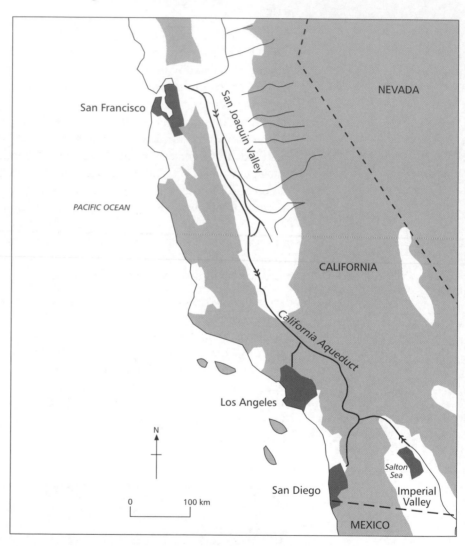

Review

3 What are the main irrigation techniques?

4 Outline the main problems associated with irrigation.

The main environmental impacts of irrigation, not just in California but in other parts of the dry Tropics, include:

- surface subsidence due to groundwater abstraction
- the loss of natural arid and semi-arid environments
- the attraction of large urban and rural populations and resulting pollution

- the introduction of new animal and plant species
- interference with the movement of animals due to canals and communication barriers
- increased salinity of soils
- water losses from host rivers.

Mineral exploitation

Mineral wealth is something that has attracted people to arid and semi-arid regions. That wealth ranges from salt to precious metals and stones. The dry Tropics account for over 80 per cent of the world's salt and copper supplies and 90 per cent of global gold. Arid regions are generally remote from markets and lack the labour, energy and water required for mineral processing. Infrastructure is limited and this increases the capital cost. Therefore, in order to be economically viable, resources must be of high quality. On the other hand, land is initially cheap, there are few local residents to object and pollution risks can be ignored. High costs mean that many mineral developments are marginal and close rapidly if the market price for the commodity falls. This has been a particular problem with copper. Precious stones and gold tend to attract 'boom and bust' developments, which do not give rise to sustained urban or industrial growth. In contrast, oil reserves have been successful in bringing sustained wealth to arid regions, particularly in the Middle East.

Case study: Oil in the Middle East

Oil was discovered in the Gulf States in the 1930s and was initially exploited for export before spawning a complex urban industrial and service economy. After the Second World War, demand increased prices, stimulating extraction and processing. Before oil, these were poor states with small populations, surviving on irrigated agriculture and trade. In many locations, such as Bahrain, drilling for oil resulted in the discovery of water-bearing strata that could be exploited for groundwater.

In addition, oil wealth provided capital for a modern infrastructure and improved port facilities, thus reducing remoteness. Wealth and the demand for water from expanding urban industrial concentrations led to the construction of desalinisation plants that transform sea water into pure water. Expensive desalinated water can support larger urban populations, employed in industry and services, and despite the arid and hostile environment, states such as Dubai or Bahrain have reached high levels of personal affluence.

Figure 5.4 Flares burn off waste gases in a desert environment

The extraction of minerals has had a number of environmental impacts. Mineral processing can be extremely toxic. This applies particularly to copper: a smelter can adversely affect vegetation 20 km downwind. Because of low population densities, there has not been quite the same pressure to introduce pollution controls to restrain such environmentally unfriendly activities, including the growth of urban areas associated with the extraction of minerals. Pipelines, roads and oil terminals also fragment the natural environment and directly affect fauna. Oil spills on land and sea have had devastating effects on fragile ecosystems.

SECTION D

Desertification

Desertification is a relative increase in the proportion of the Earth's surface classified as desert. More specifically, it refers to the encroachment of deserts into areas once considered as semi-arid or semi-arid into humid into semi-arid (**5.5**). Desertification is a major issue and has three main causes:

- a global shift in climate that is part of natural climatic change
- global warming and the greenhouse effect
- human changes to natural environments.

It is the last of these that interests us here.

With increasing population pressure, poorer agricultural populations are often pushed on to increasingly marginal land. This process of displacement has occurred in Asia, Africa and North and South America, and is directly linked with desertification. Semi-arid environments are extremely fragile, as the vegetation plays a crucial role in maintaining an

Figure 5.5 Longitudinal dune encroaching on a semi-arid area

equilibrium. Population increases place vegetation under pressure, as it is consumed by animals and used in construction and as fuel. The reduction or removal of this cover causes the surface to become mobile, triggering a progressive change as sand chokes adjacent vegetation. This leads to the formation of deflation hollows and dunes. The dry soil is rapidly lost and this prevents the re-establishment of vegetation after subsequent rain. The percentage of rainfall becoming surface run-off is increased and this encourages more soil erosion. Gullying is a frequent consequence and may lead to the formation of 'dust bowls' or 'badlands'. This complex system tends to be progressive and leads to the formation of desert environments (**5.6**).

Case study: The Dust Bowl of the American Mid-West

Agricultural colonisation of the Great Plains of North America using rain-fed cropping dates from the 1860s. Initially, droughts between 1870 and 1890 reduced yields, but colonisation and expansion of the cultivated area continued until the 1930s. By 1936, much of Kansas and Oklahoma had become an environmental disaster zone, with clouds of fine dust (soil) obscuring the Sun and spreading as far north as Chicago. In 1937, the Soil Conservation Service estimated that 43 per cent of the area at the heart of the Dust Bowl had suffered severe damage from aeolian erosion. The combination of drought and falling yields bankrupted many farming families and land was abandoned. Increased flooding and the scouring of slopes by newly formed gullies compounded the environmental damage.

Drought and wind are not unusual in this region. However, the main cause of this disaster was a combination of arable farming and recession.

Figure 5.6 Desertification
as a system

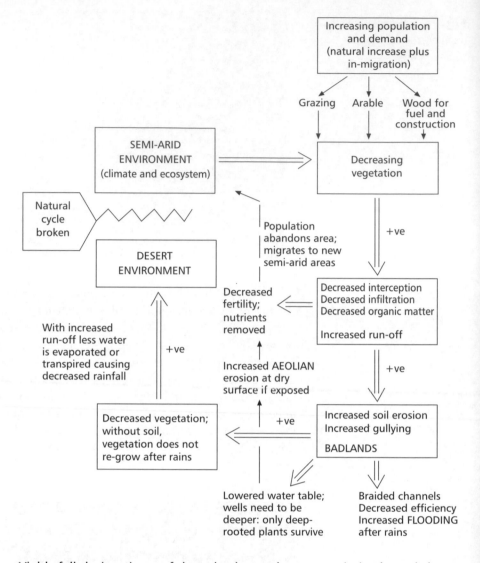

Yields fall during times of drought, but as long as grain is planted the surface remains protected from the wind. In the 1930s, however, a global recession reduced grain prices and marginal farmers could not afford to sow. The fields were left fallow, exposing the weakened topsoil to the ravages of the wind.

One effect of the social, economic and environmental disaster in the Dust Bowl was to increase public and government environmental awareness. The establishment of the Tennessee Valley Authority in the 1930s was the first large-scale attempt to manage the total environment. It helped to develop techniques to control gullying and wind erosion in semi-arid regions. Attitudes that used to regard land use as being the right of the owner changed, and a more socially responsible system developed, with Federal controls. However, the Dust Bowl also illustrates the significance of government investment and organisation. Unhappily, such intervention rarely happens in Third World countries.

Desertification is generally seen as resulting from a misuse of land rather than as an unavoidable consequence of land use. There are some fairly simple ways of avoiding it:

- **Agricultural techniques** – not leaving surfaces exposed to the atmosphere, particularly during extremely dry or wet times of the year, either by maintaining ground cover plants or leaving stubble. The construction of embankments and the planting of belts of vegetation reduces wind speeds and localises sheet wash.
- **Grazing control** – semi-arid areas have a low carrying capacity and grazing should cease before the vegetation is destroyed. In Australia a centralised service, using satellite technology, monitors sensitive areas, identifies areas of over-grazing and notifies ranchers to move their animals to areas that have been identified as offering richer pasture. In developing countries, such systems are not available and competition and short-term strategies often dominate grazing practices.
- **Fuel and construction materials** – scarce trees in semi-arid areas are often important wind breaks but are also under threat for fuel and construction materials. Demand for fuel is a major cause of Third World deforestation and the provision of more efficient cooking devices is one solution, although limited by cost.
- **Education** – local populations are aware of the causes and risks of desertification, but are not in the position to respond to long-term strategies. The cycle of poverty, in which profits from good seasons are wiped out in drought years rather than being invested in long-term projects, is difficult to break. Only governments can provide long-term investment, but their priorities often lie in the urban and industrial centres.

Degraded land tends to form a vicious cycle of deterioration that is difficult to control, let alone to improve or return to the original state. Many present semi-arid landscapes formed under past, more humid conditions. Once the balance between soils and vegetation is breached, it becomes extremely difficult to re-establish vegetation without soil – and it is impossible to re-establish soil without vegetation. In effect, a primary succession will not occur. Instead, a new equilibrium of aridity is established.

Two main techniques can be used to reverse desertification, although high costs limit their application:

- **Stabilisation of the surface** – before vegetation can establish, the surface must be stabilised to prevent drifting material smothering new plants and to allow nutrients to be stored. In extreme cases, crude oil is poured on the surface around plants to act as a cement, but more generally the focus is on wind breaks to reduce surface velocity.
- **Run-off control** – gullies become part of the drainage system and half-hearted attempts to fill them in merely provide greater load during the next rains. Repair is expensive, as only large stones and gabions (mesh boxes filled with small stones) have sufficient energy to withstand

7 Explain what is meant by the term **desertification**, and examine its main causes.

8 Why are semi-arid environments so fragile?

9 Describe and explain the ways in which semi-arid environments can be exploited in a sustainable manner.

run-off. Diversion drains are used where possible, but these are costly and require careful planning if they are not to cause further damage elsewhere.

So, to sum up, semi-arid regions tend to be more sensitive to human-induced change than deserts. Vegetation plays a critical role in controlling more vigorous geomorphological processes. Semi-arid lands are more attractive to human populations: they have a greater agricultural potential and they are often sparsely populated, which offers the possibility of land ownership. The sustainable use of these areas by a significant population is demanding, and the most frequent consequence is land degradation and the movement of population to new areas or to the cities.

Enquiry

1 Select one hot desert region that has been settled and irrigated for agriculture.
   a How has water been provided to allow agriculture?
   b What are the main markets for the crops produced?
   c What problems have been encountered?
   d To what extent is the chosen scheme sustainable?

2 Select one mineral resource development in an arid or semi-arid region.
   a Draw a map to show the location of the mineral resource, the main settlements, communications and processing facilities.
   b Briefly outline and explain the main environmental impact of the resource development on the surrounding environment.
   c To what extent was the provision of infrastructure for the resource development a problem?
   d What is the benefit of the resource development to the local population?

3 Select one example of desertification that you have studied.
   a Draw a systems diagram to show the main causes and consequences of desertification in your example (use **5.6** as a starting-point).
   b What measures have been taken in your example to stop or reverse the process?
   c Explain why these measures should be effective.
   d Given that the causes and consequences of desertification are well established, why does it still occur in the world today?

The humid Tropics

Climatic characteristics

Between the discontinuous zones of aridity lie some of the wettest regions in the world. The transition from desert to 'rain all year' is gradual and is generally expressed in terms of the balance between wet and dry seasons. Adjacent to hot deserts, semi-arid regions (Köppen BS or steppe climate) have a short rainy season, and as the duration of the rains increases, tropical grassland or savanna climates (Aw) develop (**1.2**). Extremely seasonal climate, with high rainfall occurring in a short time, is referred to as monsoon climate (Am), as in the Bay of Bengal. Along the Equator and extending to latitude 25° over the Pacific, the equatorial climate is characterised by high humidity and high temperatures, with little seasonal variation (Af). Precipitation is well distributed throughout the year, with annual totals of over 2500 mm. Diurnal and seasonal temperature ranges are small (**1.5**). The remarkable temperature pattern for Altamira (3°S 52°W) shows little deviation from the average, producing a constant and monotonous regime (**6.1**).

Figure 6.1 Temperature variation at Altamira

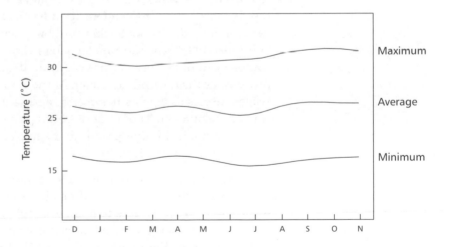

The Köppen climate classification includes reference to vegetation, so that the increase in precipitation is generally reflected in a progression from desert, through scrub, tropical grassland and dry forest to tropical rain forest. This sequence is particularly clear in North Africa, between the Sahara Desert and the Congo Basin. The main factor controlling the pattern of precipitation is the location of the intertropical convergence zone (ITCZ) but, locally, ocean currents and relief can be important.

Equable temperatures

In theory, equatorial regions should experience eight seasons a year. In practice, these are seldom evident. The movement of the Earth in relation to the Sun means that on the Equator the Sun is overhead at noon twice a year (21 March and 21 September – the Equinoxes). Even when maximum insolation lies over the Tropics (the solstices), temperatures at the Equator remain high. It is just possible to identify two 'peaks' in the average temperature for Altamira in October and March (although these are only 1–2°C hotter than the average). Equability of temperature is further increased by the high humidity and the high frequency of cloud cover, which traps heat at the surface. In the Amazon and Congo Basins, relief isolates the local system from global circulation patterns. In the Amazon Basin, approximately half of the precipitation is derived from local evapotranspiration.

Heavy rainfall

Why does it rain so frequently in the humid Tropics? The equatorial belt forms a fairly continuous zone of low pressure. The air at the surface is hotter and less dense than the surrounding (environmental) air and it rises in convective cells. As the air rises, it expands and this causes adiabatic cooling. This temperature change is initially at the dry adiabatic lapse rate (DALR) of 1°C per 100 m and it reduces the air's ability to hold water vapour. As the air cools, its relative humidity increases and at 100 per cent the water vapour in the air condenses to form cloud droplets. The temperature at which this occurs is called the **dew point** and the base of the cloud is termed the **condensation level**. During condensation, latent heat is released, causing further instability with the air continuing to cool at 0.5° per 100 m (the saturated adiabatic lapse rate, or SALR). Ascent continues until the local air has cooled to the same temperature and pressure as the environmental air. At the Equator, this point of stability, or **tropopause**, is as high as 16 km and represents the maximum height of cloud development. These clouds develop as individual convection cells (or storms) and it is this that produced the line of circular globular (cumuliform) clouds visible on **2.3**.

The equatorial zone not only has a high number of rain days, but the rain often has a high intensity. Rain droplets reach a large size (4.0 mm in diameter, in comparison to temperate droplets of approximately 1.5 mm) as droplet formation is enhanced in the towering clouds. The terminal velocity of large raindrops is as high as 950 cm s^{-1}, in comparison with temperate droplets that reach 450 cm s^{-1}. The height of cloud development is determined by surface energy, and within these towering cumulonimbus clouds small cloud droplets (0.01–0.04 mm in diameter) fuse around hygroscopic nuclei to form water droplets with a sufficient mass to fall towards the surface as precipitation. The conversion of cloud droplets to water droplets is complex and is thought to involve two main types of process: coalescence and the Bergeron–Findeisen process.

The coalescence, or collision, process relates to the turbulence found in towering clouds. As cloud droplets are moved upwards in thermals and downwards in down-draughts, they collide and fuse to increase in mass. These start to fall within the cloud and further collision causes the growing water droplets to become unstable and divide, continuing the process. Clouds at the ITCZ may be over 15 km in height and contain powerful air currents to cause significant coalescence.

The Bergeron–Findeisen process focuses on the role of ice in the formation of precipitation. During ascent, air with a temperature of 25–30°C at the surface cools to well below freezing point. Indeed, at the tropopause, air may be as cold as −75°C and the cloud is largely composed of ice crystals. Cloud droplets do not freeze as soon as the temperature falls below freezing unless nuclei are present, and these tend to be less common than cloud droplets. The middle and lower parts of a cumulonimbus cloud contain a mixture of super-cooled water droplets and ice crystals. The crystals literally grow by a process of accretion as water vapour in the air is condensed and frozen on to their surfaces. Typically, the ice crystals develop into snowflakes or hail stones and these fall towards the surface, melting before they reach to ground to form large rain droplets.

Review

1 What is meant by the **equatorial low-pressure belt**. How does it form?

2 Why is relative humidity so high in the equatorial zone?

3 What effect does cloud cover have on temperature at low latitudes?

4 Check that you understand the coalescence and Bergeron–Findeisen processes.

Processes in the humid Tropics

From the air, tropical rain forests present a vista of a uniform canopy broken by large meandering rivers. In many respects, the vegetation acts as a barrier between the atmosphere and the lithosphere, so that most geomorphological processes occur beneath the surface. It is only when the vegetation is disturbed that surface activity becomes apparent.

Weathering and mass movement

The constant high temperatures and abundant supply of water mean high rates of chemical weathering. Water acts as the medium for most reactions, and rates at least double with every 10°C increase in temperature. Where rocks are permeable or pervious, chemical weathering occurs to great depths and the **basal surface of weathering** (the junction between **regolith** and consolidated rock) is often deeper than 100 m. The main processes are **hydration** and **hydrolysis** (see pages 18–19) and give rise to large quantities of sand and hydrated clays, including bauxite. The uneven distribution of joints in igneous rocks gives rise to major variations in the depth of regolith that are not reflected in topography. Limestone weathers rapidly through **carbonation** and produces extensive underground systems of caves and rivers, including **tower karst** (south-east China) and **cockpit karst** (Jamaica).

The potential for mass movements in tropical humid environments is high (**2.5a**):

- The stress force is increased by the weight of water saturating the soil and the regolith.
- The deep weathering and accumulation of unconsolidated regolith reduce the cohesive force.
- The frictional force is decreased by lubrication from rain.

However, within the rain forest mass movement is not common, as the surface is covered and consolidated by vegetation. The root systems of the closely spaced trees effectively bind the soil to the regolith and the regolith to the bedrock, so that slopes as steep as 60° and with a deep soil cover can remain stable. It is only where the vegetation cover is broken, as along the banks of rivers, that slope failure is evident. Under unusually heavy rainfall, even stable forested slopes can fail, as occurred in Honduras and Guatemala during hurricane Mitch in 1998, after as much as 6000 mm of rain fell in 36 hours.

Erosion

Fluvial processes dominate in rain forest environments, but rivers are not as active as might be expected given the extremely high rainfall (**6.2**). The Amazon has by far the largest discharge of the world's rivers (200 000 cumecs) and returns approximately one-third of all fresh water to the sea (**6.3**). With its mass, the Amazon is the most efficient river in the world, with an hydraulic radius (the cross-sectional area divided by the wetted perimeter) in excess of 50 even at Manaus and a cross-section that dwarfs that of the Mississippi (**6.4**). The paradox is that despite enormous energy, the Amazon does not carry a proportionate load. The mouth of the river has no delta and in terms of suspended load it is one of the cleanest major rivers in the world. As the Amazon is the only major artery removing material from the basin, this implies that rates of denudation in the region are relatively low.

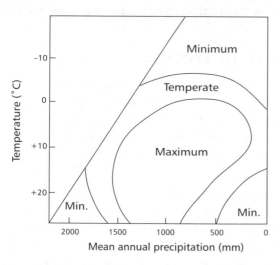

Figure 6.2 The Peltier diagram of fluvial processes

Figure 6.3 The characteristics of ten large rivers

River	Drainage area (10^3 km²)	Length (km)	Water discharge (m³/s)	Water discharge (km³/yr)	Sediment discharge (10^3 t/yr)
Amazon	6150	6275	200 000	6300	900 000
Zaire (Congo)	3820	4670	40 000	1250	43 000
Orinoco	990	2570	34 880	1100	210 000
Ganges–Brahmaputra	1480	2700	30 790	971	1 670 000
Yangtse	1940	4990	28 540	900	478 000
Mississippi–Missouri	3270	6260	18 390	580	210 000
Yenisei	2580	5710	17 760	560	13 000
Lena	2500	4600	16 300	514	12 000
Mekong	790	4180	14 900	470	160 000
Parana–La Plata	2830	3940	?14 900	?470	92 000

Figure 6.4 Cross-sections of the Amazon (at Manaus) and the Mississippi (mouth)

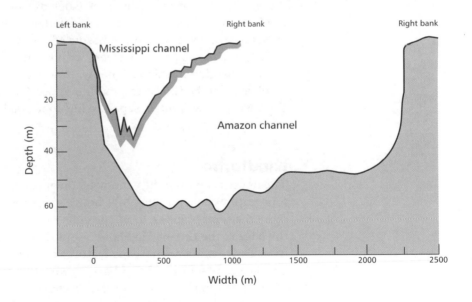

Why fluvial erosion is relatively weak in tropical humid environments is an intriguing question. Tropical rain forests provide a graphic illustration of the powerful role of vegetation.

The tree canopy intercepts intense rainfall and both breaks the impact of the large water droplets and reduces the rate at which they reach the surface. Rainfall is temporarily stored on leaf surfaces before it runs down branches and stems (**stem-flow**), or drips to the ground (**leaf-drip**):

- A significant proportion of the water evaporates off the leaves back into the atmosphere.
- Water reaches the surface over a greater time period than the rain event, reducing rainfall intensity.
- The surface is always moist and is rich in shallow root systems. Infiltration is extremely efficient and the infiltration capacity is in excess of the intercepted precipitation intensity. Direct surface run-off only occurs after periods of prolonged rain, when the whole forest floor floods.
- The root systems form a continuous surface cover, preventing channels from forming. The drainage density in tropical rain forests is low, with few small streams. Rather, water reaches the large channels as throughflow, interflow or base flow through the deep regolith.
- The infiltrated water absorbs minerals but it does not pick up a significant load in suspension. The vegetation holds the particles of clay, silt and sand in place and inhibits fluvial erosion.
- This is a system of negative feedback, as although high precipitation provides the energy for fluvial erosion it also sustains abundant vegetation that reduces the effectiveness of fluvial erosion.

The sediment yield of tropical rain forest rivers illustrates the processes occurring in specific drainage basins. In the Amazon system, tributaries that drain areas of crystalline rock (such as the Rio Negro, which drains the Guiana Highlands) tend to be black due to their high organic load. In contrast, tributaries that drain basins of weaker sedimentary rocks (such as the upper Amazon, or 'milk-river', with an Andean catchment) tend to be cloudy with clay and silt sediments. Downstream of Manaus, below the confluence of the Rio Negro and the upper Amazon (**6.5**), the two contrasting flows remain separate for up to 100 km and even support distinctive fish populations.

Landforms

The impression from the canopy of a plain is often deceptive, as the topography is often rolling hills between extensive flood plains. In areas of more resistant granites, dramatic cliffs may emerge – as, for example, at the edge of the Guiana Highlands – but these areas of exposed rock are rare. The dominant landscape features are meandering river channels, ox-bow lakes, cut-offs and point bars, as well as braiding where local steeping of the river long profile occurs. River courses are often convoluted, complex and rapidly changing (**6.5**).

On the flood plains, the forest adjacent to the channel is seasonally flooded (in Brazil this is termed the **varzea**) and as the water subsides the saturated and unsupported banks often collapse, with the bank-edge vegetation toppling in to the water. During flooding, a significant discharge passes through the forest, transporting sediment and organic material into cut-offs and ox-bow lakes as well as cutting new channels. The frequency of abandoned river features is high (see **6.5**) and these areas are colonised by

Figure 6.5 An aerial view of flood plain features above the confluence of the Rio Negro (upper) and the Solimões (lower) at Manaus, Brazil. The abandoned channels, cut-offs, ox-bow lakes and marsh are clearly visible in the varzea zone adjacent to the main channels. The high discharge of the main channels often 'dams' tributaries, creating lakes. The deposition that this causes is evident on the Rio Negro as braids.

aquatic vegetation in a rapid sequence of primary succession that produces areas of high fertility with nutrient rich soils. With rapid meandering and seasonal flooding, the development of point bars is a noticeable feature, with extensive ridges of cobble, gravel and sand occurring on the inside of meanders. When rivers drain granite areas, extensive banks and bars of sand – consisting of sediment released by the hydrolysis of feldspar in the bedrock – are exposed during periods of low flow.

Away from the rivers, the topography reflects the underlying rock lithology and structure, although the geology is generally hidden by a vegetation-protected deep layer of regolith. Stream density is generally low and channels are often deeply incised. The infiltration capacity of the surface is high due to both the vegetation and the regolith, but where streams have developed they rapidly cut down through the low-resistance surface regolith. Such deep valleys are closed over by the canopy and are seldom evident from the air. Despite the high rainfall, rates of denudation are generally lower than in temperate environments and there is generally little evidence of mass movement or sheet wash within the forest.

In conclusion, the humid tropical region forms the powerhouse of global atmospheric circulation and a sustained belt of low pressure with instability and a high rainfall. Rates of weathering are high, but mass movement and fluvial erosion are generally weak unless the vegetation cover has been disturbed. This makes tropical forest surfaces potentially fragile and vulnerable, threatening the release of extremely large quantities of unconsolidated material as well as modifying regional climates.

5 Why does regolith accumulate to such depths in tropical humid environments?

6 Why is mass movement relatively infrequent under tropical rain forest cover?

7 With reference to **6.3**, write a explanatory account comparing the Amazon with one of the top five rivers.

8 How might river discharge data be used to assess rates of deforestation in the drainage basin?

9 Describe how rates of weathering, mass movement and erosion would be affected by removal of forest cover.

10 To what extent can tropical humid environments be regarded as geomorphologically inactive?

Enquiry

1 Select one major river draining a region of tropical rain forest.
   a Draw a diagram to show the drainage basin, the main types of vegetation and the main settlements.
   b Annotate the map to show areas of forest clearance, road construction or expansion of settlements.
   c Describe and explain the likely changes in discharge (at the mouth of the river) as deforestation in the basin increases.
   d Identify likely changes in load characteristics after extensive deforestation.
   e Explain the implications of the load changes for both fluvial landforms and settlement in the lower valley.

2 With reference to a major meteorological event (hurricane, monsoon, typhoon or tropical storm):
   a Write a brief description of the event, including details of the level of precipitation and the human costs.
   b Explain why such events are common in your chosen area.
   c Outline the problems of predicting and managing such events in your chosen area.
   d Examine the differences between the short- and long-term effects of the chosen event.
   e Assess the extent to which human activity magnified the event.
   f What steps might be taken to minimise the impact of such events in your chosen area?

Tropical rain forests

Soils

Soils are a synthesis of organic and inorganic matter. In tropical humid climates, where both constituents are in abundance, the soils that develop can only be regarded with surprise. A typical tropical rain forest soil has a thin topsoil, and is low in nutrient content, poorly sorted and relatively infertile. The zonal soil group is referred to as **laterite** or **latisol** and the basic characteristics are shown in **7.1**. These soils are partially studied or mapped, and the uniform vegetation cover hides a considerable variety of soil types.

Figure 7.1 A generalised profile of a tropical humid soil

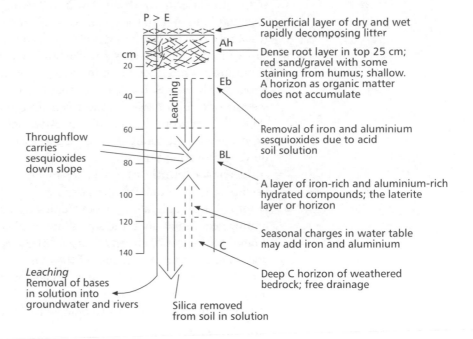

Tropical humid soils tend to share four main characteristics (**7.1**):

■ **Acidity** Tropical forest soils are naturally acidic. With precipitation greater than evaporation, the dominant movement of water is downwards and this removes bases in solution (**leaching**). Infiltrating water gains acidity from organic acids that are released as organic matter decomposes, thus forming an acidic soil solution. Through cation exchange, hydrogen in the soil solution is exchanged with nutrients stored on clay and humus particles. The nutrients are removed in solution into groundwater, and eventually into rivers. Over time, this causes a build-up of hydrogen in the soil, increasing acidity and the loss of nutrients from the soil. This results in a loss of fertility. With precipitation frequently over 3000 mm and evaporation of approximately 350 mm, leaching is a dominant process in the humid Tropics.

■ **Depth** Tropical humid soils often develop on deep accumulations of regolith and have extended B and C horizons of up to 100 m. The subsoil dominates, with slightly modified weathered parent material. It is this that determines the soil colour, the brown/black staining of humus usually being absent. This allows large volumes of precipitation to infiltrate before the soil reaches saturation and reduces rates of surface run-off.

■ **Iron concentrations** Latisols are frequently red in colour, indicating an accumulation of ferric compounds. The acidic soil water breaks down clay particles into silica and sesquioxides (iron and aluminium compounds in clay). Under high temperatures, the silica is moved downwards while the sesquioxides are retained in the upper soil. This process is termed **ferrallitisation**. This produces a relatively infertile soil, as the laterite horizon is low in nutrients and concentrated iron is toxic to plants. When the soil is exposed and dries, it produces a resistant crust and breaks down to form a fine red dust which is susceptible to aeolian erosion. The surface accumulation of iron and aluminium is often too great to have just originated from clay in the upper soil horizons. It is thought that there is a lateral movement of sesquioxides in solution, as these soils frequently occur at the base of slopes where groundwater collects. After deforestation, the surface is exposed to direct sunlight, causing increased evaporation and the upward movement of groundwater. This produces a red, iron-rich surface layer (**plinthite**) that bakes to a hard crust in dry periods and becomes sticky mud after heavy rain.

■ **Humus** Although fall-out from tropical forest vegetation is high, humus accumulation in the soil is low. Typically, organic matter is limited to the top 10 cm and there is little incorporation into the lower horizons. This occurs because of the extremely rapid breakdown of surface organic matter and the rapid leaching of organic material. At the base of slopes or in poorly drained areas (in particular, abandoned river channels), peaty soils develop, with far greater concentrations of organic material.

Review

1 Try to explain what is meant by the term **soil fertility**.

2 Explain why tropical humid soils:

■ tend to have a low content of organic matter
■ are often rich in iron and aluminium.

3 Why is leaching such a vigorous process in tropical humid soils?

The structure of the rain forest

Rain forests contain a bewildering variety of flora and fauna but do share some important characteristics, and there is a common set of concerns.

Key

A Emergent canopy – discontinuous

B Middle canopy – discontinuous

C Lower canopy – continuous/dense

D Saplings

E Sparse ground cover

Figure 7.2 The vertical structure of the tropical rain forest

Structure

Structure is the spatial organisation and arrangement of the forest and, in particular, the vertical and horizontal patterns of flora and fauna. Rain forests are characterised by a distinctive **vertical organisation** of flora, referred to as canopies (**7.2**).

- The **emergent canopy** is discontinuous and consists of mature trees with straight **boles** (trunks). Trees can reach 50 m and typically have umbrella-shaped crowns and buttress roots, to help maintain stability. The canopy often contains a highly specialised saprophytic plant community, which uses host trees to gain access to sunlight. The saprophytes are also specialised in both retaining water and withstanding ultra-violet radiation, as the upper canopy dries out rapidly between rain events.
- The **middle canopy** consists of a continuous belt of large mature trees of between 20 and 30 m in height. These have mop-shaped crowns and the branches intermingle and are linked by lianas, providing mutual support. This zone is rich in foliage and fruit. It is the ecological niche for numerous insect, bird and animal species that will rarely, if ever, venture to the forest floor. The emergent canopy offers protection to the middle canopy from wind gusts and intense rain and drying. The protection is generally at least 90 per cent effective.
- The **lower canopy** consists of densely packed conical shaped trees. This layer is protected from intense sunlight and intense rain by the upper and middle canopies. Humidity is generally high. Rich in food, this canopy provides a major niche for fauna.
- The **shrub canopy** reaches approximately 5 m from the ground. It is discontinuous, with plants such as palms, banana and ferns, that are specialised in having large chlorophyll-rich leaves that can exploit the heavily filtered sunlight. Rain reaches this layer as a mist or gentle

drip. Saplings, from the seeds of the adjacent trees, have a short life span due to the lack of sunlight, unless the upper canopies are punctured.

- **Ground cover** is generally limited and discontinuous due to shading by the canopies. The forest floor is often dark and has a more limited fauna than the tree canopies, with insects and decomposers dominating.

- The **root mat** forms a dense and tangled floor to the forest. The close spacing of the tree trunks means that root systems overlap, forming a ribbed surface. This efficiently protects the underlying regolith and soil, as well as serving as a filter to trap nutrients as soon as they are released by the decomposition of leaves, branches and trunks that litter the floor. Rain forest trees have a very high above-ground to below-ground ratio of tissue (at least 4 : 1), so that most of the energy is invested in productive tissue.

The **horizontal distribution** of species in tropical rain forests has three main features.

The **diversity** is the number of species found within a specific area. The total number of tree species remains an estimate, although the Amazon Basin contains over 2500 species of tall trees; over 1000 species are found in Pará State alone. A sample area of one hectare may contain up to 80 species (compared with a value of 35 for temperate deciduous forest). But diversity increases as the sample area increases. In a 1.5 ha area more than 120 species can be found, and in 2 ha over 175. No one dominant species tends to develop, so the forest continually varies. The high diversity is thought to reflect both high rates of mutation and the role of past climate. There is one theory that during the Quaternary period, the tropical rain forests fragmented into small areas separated by tropical savanna. Small enclaves of forest evolved separately and developed different characteristics. Under rising temperatures at the end of the Quaternary, the pockets re-merged, creating the present diverse pattern. In contrast, **mosaic theory** focuses on the consistent pattern of saplings not being related to the species that they are growing under. Thus, when canopy trees die, they are seldom replaced by the same species, which makes for dynamic change over time and space.

The **spatial patterns** of particular tree species tend not to show concentrations. Rather, on average, individual specimens are over 2 km apart. This is particularly hard to explain in a system in which high humidity and the dense packing of trees limit dispersal of seed by wind. Explanations focus on the role of pests. The combination of temperature, water and a large biomass provides a rich ecological niche for bacteria, viruses, insects, herbivores and omnivores, making the humid Tropics a very hostile environment. Specialisation by pests to tolerate specific tree defences has resulted in tree-specific pest populations. As concentrations of a tree species develop over time, the food supply for the specific pest increases, leading to a dramatic increase in the pest population. This multiplication of population eventually exceeds the carrying capacity and so the destruction of the entire tree concentration begins.

Rain forest vegetation shows a wide range of adaptation strategies that allow survival in a highly competitive and hostile environment:

- **Growth rates** In an environment with strong competition for light, rapid vertical growth allows saplings to exploit access to sunlight provided by any gap in the canopy. Vines and lianas use existing trees to reach sunlight. Lacking large trunks, some – such as the fig vine – eventually strangle and kill the host tree, forming a vertical chimney of interlocking stems. Figs illustrate the complexity of adaptation, as the plant is established from a wind-blown seed and grows as a small bush at the junction of an upper branch and the trunk. It then produces aerial roots, with some coiling around the trunk and some descending vertically to root in the soil. This source of water and nutrients allows the bush to grow upwards, and eventually to shade and kill the host tree. One species of palm tree even has a symbiotic relationship with leaf-cutting ants, so that in 'exchange' for residence in the trunk, the ants clear a forest patch, allowing the palm access to light.

- **Height** Although not the tallest trees in the world (the sequoia of North American coniferous forests reaches 110 m), rain forest species reach over 60 m, with an average of 45–55 m. Trunks tend to have relatively small **girths** (diameters), although taller species tend to have buttress roots to increase stability. The dense packing and the growth of vines between trees increase stability; energy is not wasted in growing deep root systems.

- **Root systems** Feeding roots (**tendrils**) are concentrated near the surface. They are highly efficient at absorbing nutrients and water, with 80 per cent of roots in the top 25 cm of the soil. Specialised fungi (**mycorrhiza**) play an important role in accelerating the decomposition of organic matter and its absorption by roots. Few roots penetrate into the deep regolith, as there are few nutrients, and a copious supply of water to the upper soil reduces the need for tap roots to exploit groundwater.

- **Leaves** Leaves are vulnerable to the impact of rain, wind and pests. The weight of water in a tropical downpour poses a threat to branches and leaves, and adaptations include large ribs, a V-shape to channel water off rapidly, a waxy cuticle to reduce surface tension and extended leaf points to increase drip-flow. To reduce attack by pests, plants have developed extraordinary defences, ranging from alkaloid poisons to thick cuticles and thorns.

- **Reproduction** Wind dispersal of seeds is only efficient for upper canopy plants above the high humidity and shelter of the lower layers. Many plants produce fruits that are consumed by animals and then 'deposited' at a distance, giving fauna an important role in the maintenance of the forest systems. Plants growing adjacent to rivers, or in areas prone to flooding, use water as means of transmission.

Review

4 Briefly define the terms **biome, forest structure** and **ecosystem**.

5 Explain what is meant by 'competition' between plant species.

6 Why do more canopy layers develop in tropical rain forests than in other forest ecosystems?

The functioning of the rain forest

Function refers to the processes or flows that occur between the components (structure) of the system. With an average 45 kg of biomass per square metre, the rain forest provides an abundant supply of food in numerous ecological niches. Each layer of the rain forest can be considered as an ecosystem (often in relative isolation); the same may be true even of individual tree species. One recent attempt fully to document all biota in a few hectares of rain forest in Thailand was abandoned when it became apparent that it would have required 20 per cent of all taxonomists in the world to complete the task! In Amazonia, there are over 1800 known species of butterfly, over 1900 species of bird, and the River Amazon contains over 2000 species of fish (compared with 250 for the Mississippi).

The quantification of relatively large organisms is demanding enough, but insects are even more difficult to collect and identify. In Thailand's forests, over 350 insects can be collected in a square metre (this includes all vertical levels) and a fair proportion of them would be new to science. In addition to their intrinsic value, fauna plays a vital role in plant reproduction, species dispersal and the recycling of organic matter. It is the intense micro-organism activity that allows the rapid transmission of nutrients through the litter and soil, and it is this that sustains such rapid vegetation growth.

The functioning of an ecosystem is generally investigated through the **nutrient cycle**, **trophic levels** and **food webs**.

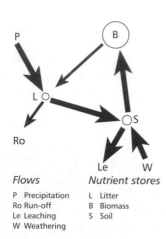

Flows

P Precipitation
Ro Run-off
Le Leaching
W Weathering

Nutrient stores

L Litter
B Biomass
S Soil

Figure 7.3 A generalised tropical forest nutrient cycle: flows and stores are shown proportionally

The nutrient cycle

In the humid Tropics, vegetation functions relatively independently of soil-creating activity. In this respect, the nutrient cycle is unusual (**7.3**).

- The biomass is the main nutrient store (approximately 70 per cent by dry weight), with fairly insignificant amounts in the litter and soil. This reflects both the large scale of the vegetation and the extremely rapid rates of decomposition at the surface. Nutrients remain trapped in the biomass until either trees die or the forest is cleared and burnt.
- Nutrient flows are large due to the temperatures and precipitation, maintaining high rates of growth, decay and transport.
- Precipitation is shown as providing a large nutrient supply to the litter. Nutrients are added as the water passes through decomposing vegetation lodged in the canopies (much of the dead organic matter does not reach the forest floor).
- The soil acts as a routeway rather than as a store. Nutrients released from the litter or from weathering are either taken up by plants or are lost through leaching rather than accumulating in the soil.
- The litter store is small, as organic matter has either decomposed before reaching the litter or is rapidly broken down or consumed on the forest floor. Typically, the surface has only a thin layer of fall-out and there is no significant organic horizon.

- The usual roles of litter and soil are redundant, as the vegetation is specialised to re-circulate nutrients rapidly. With weak seasonality, the decomposition of organic matter is constant, providing a continuous flow of nutrients for the vegetation. Equally, regular rainfall reduces the need for the soil to store water. This highly efficient recycling allows rain forest to develop on variable surfaces, including abandoned roads or concrete!
- Fall-out is well distributed, as in the absence of seasons trees have independent cycles. Leaf fall is determined by pest and wind damage rather than by climate.

Trophic levels

The relationship between organisms in an ecosystem can be thought of as a sequence of energy transfers or flows. This can be represented as a hierarchy, divided into levels by status (**7.4**).

Figure 7.4 The classic trophic levels

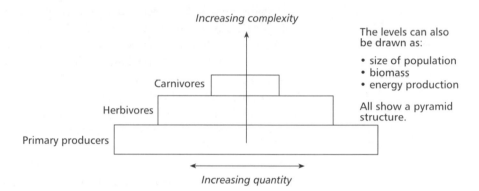

- The base of the hierarchy forms the origin of the energy that supports all higher levels. These organisms, almost totally flora, are termed **primary producers**, as they combine carbon dioxide, water and sunlight through **photosynthesis** to produce carbohydrates, including cellulose. The level of photosynthesis is generally measured by **net primary productivity** (NPP), which quantifies the total energy fixed by plants minus the energy used for respiration and tissue repair. This is measured in terms of dry weight of biomass as $kg\ m^{-2}\ yr^{-1}$ and the high NPP of rain forests ($2.2\ kg\ m^{-2}\ yr^{-1}$) supports large higher trophic levels.
- A wide range of organisms, including insects, bacteria and fungi, consume the tissue produced by photosynthesis. In rain forests, grazing animals (herbivores) do not play a major role, as much of the biomass is well above the forest floor. Tree-climbing animals do consume leaves, but these are generally omnivorous, eating a range of foods, including meat. Insects, by far the largest group of organisms, are the main consumers of the living and dead biomass.
- The wide range of organisms provides food for the upper trophic level of carnivores. This is a large and diverse population, which reflects the large food supplies, and it includes the large cats (tigers and jaguars) as

well as crocodiles, alligators and fish such as the piranha.

■ The quantity of energy stored in each trophic level decreases with increasing status. This is due to the loss of energy (heat) during conversion, when it is digested (broken down) and reassembled.

■ The upper level of carnivores is the most vulnerable to change and dominates the list of endangered species (jaguars, tigers, alligators, sloths and monkeys) in the rain forest. Changes in the lower trophic levels cause a progressive loss of food supply to the levels above as well as a loss of habitat.

Food webs (chains)

Trophic levels do not fully explain the functioning of the ecosystem. They were recognised in the investigation of temperate ecosystems, where herbivores provide the main link between primary producers and carnivores. In rain forests, there are few true herbivores and insects form the most important group of organisms consuming biomass. Insects are generally regarded as decomposers or recyclers (**7.5**). In rain forests, their role is extremely complex, being consumers of both living and dead material, as well as food for a very wide range of fauna and even some carnivorous flora. Food webs and chains only provide a crude map of energy flows in a rain forest. A combination of the immense number of species, the range of food consumed by species, the numerous micro-habitats and micro-ecosystems, as well as the interaction between riverine and terrestrial systems, makes the construction of a full web an impossible task. In such a dynamic and competitive environment, it is difficult even to separate consumers from the consumed. What is clear is that insects play a key role, and that it is these that form the major links between the organisms in the trophic hierarchy.

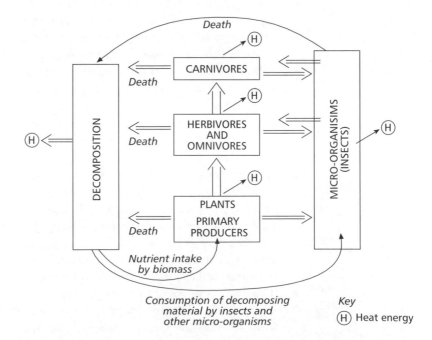

Figure 7.5 The role of insects in the tropical forest nutrient cycle

Tropical rain forests are exotic, fascinating and even threatening environments. As a topic of considerable debate and a global issue, our scientific knowledge remains unexpectedly sparse. Rain forests appear to be structured and orderly, but in practice they consist of chaotic and extremely complex systems. They also represent a major global biomass, yet they grow on relatively infertile soils, and they appear robust when in fact they are fairly fragile. Part of the problem of understanding rain forests is that ecological models do not easily fit. Concepts such as nutrient cycling, trophic levels and food webs do not really fit the more dynamic rain forest system. Even concepts such as **primary succession** are difficult to apply, as the development through **seres** to a **climatic climax vegetation** in equilibrium seems inappropriate. The structure of the rain forest implies that change is always occurring and that an equilibrium is never reached. There is no dominant tree species, and trees are not replaced by the same species. Specific trees also provide a micro-habitat for specific communities of organisms, suggesting that fauna as well as flora is in a constant state of upheaval and change. Rain forest research is still largely at a data collection stage and the task of examining these as a system remains a mammoth one for the future.

Review

7 Attempt to explain why biomass forms the largest of the nutrient stores in the rain forest system.

8 Why is the main nutrient flow into the litter store shown as precipitation rather than fall-out (**7.2**)?

9 How can the concept of **carrying capacity** be related to trophic levels?

10 Identify how a reduction in vegetation affects the number of carnivores when they do not eat biomass.

11 What are the main problems in applying the concepts of **nutrient cycling**, **trophic levels** and **food webs** to rain forest ecosystems?

12 Suggest reasons why scientific knowledge of the tropical rain forest is relatively incomplete. What are the implications of this incomplete knowledge for human use of the environment?

13 What can be done to increase our knowledge of the tropical rain forest environment?

Enquiry

Identify and investigate ways in which the tropical rain forest may justifiably be called a hostile environment.

People and the humid Tropics

Introduction

Tropical rain forests extend over 17 million km^2 and form the third most extensive biome. At over 750 billion tonnes, it is the largest in terms of weight of vegetation and is also the world's richest ecosystem, dominating the gene pools of flora and fauna. Knowledge of the rain forest remains incomplete, and the much-used phrase 'somewhere in the rain forest is a cure for cancer' sums up both the potential and the lack of knowledge of such a significant ecosystem.

Until the mid-20th century, the scale, inaccessibility and hostility of the rain forests ensured their protection. Population growth in tropical countries, its associated increase in demand for land, the expansion of communications and the rising demand for raw materials, as well as political ambition, have placed the rain forests under threat. Their survival is now a major global issue. The current rate of loss is estimated at 7.5 million ha a year, an area equivalent to the size of Luxembourg, Belgium and the Netherlands. In the Philippines, 17 million ha of rain forest have been reduced to 7 million.

Traditional use of the rain forest

For well over 10 000 years, the rain forests have supported small, often isolated groups of horticulturalists, who supplemented their food supply by hunting and gathering. They exploited the wealth of the ecosystem without apparent ecological degradation. Such groups are often heralded as models of conservation, as working examples of how sustainable exploitation of the forest is possible. To some extent, this claim is both valid and useful.

Horticulture in the rain forests of South America, Africa and Asia is based on a system known as **slash-and-burn**, or **shifting cultivation**. This involves a regular cycle of clearance, burning, planting and abandonment – and, less frequently, the movement of villages. This system is seen as showing ecological adaptation at all levels of organisation:

- Fields or gardens are small, usually feeding a household (**8.1**). The intact surrounding vegetation allows rapid regeneration of the plot, as well as giving protection from wind, rain and sun.
- Burning vegetation releases the nutrients trapped in the biomass store (**7.3**), which is rapidly washed into the soil to boost short-term fertility and sustain crop growth.

Figure 8.1 Traditional garden clearance after burning

- Gardens are left half-cleared of stumps, half-burnt trunks and branches, to protect the surface from rain and hold the fragile soil in place.
- The field is abandoned after 3–5 years, because the nutrients in the soil have been leached out and yields decline. On abandonment, the rain forest re-establishes and the nutrient cycle is restored with no lasting, adverse ecological impact.

Review

1 Explain why shifting cultivation is regarded as being well adapted to the tropical forest environment.

2 Why is the burning of vegetation so important in shifting cultivation?

3 Identify the main problems arising from shifting cultivation.

Shifting cultivation is ecologically sensitive, but its practitioners rarely justify it in these terms. The reason they give for abandoning gardens is the build-up of pests and weeds that seriously reduce yields. Villages are also moved at intervals because the thatch, rubbish and excrement attract pests and vermin. Older gardens remain in use for considerable periods for tree crops and are not fully abandoned. The main factors reducing environmental impact are the low level of technology, the small scale of the population and the distance between villages. Quite simply, a small population equipped with stone axes is not a major threat to the environment.

It is difficult to see how shifting cultivation can be applied at a more commercial scale. Low levels of technology and demand sustain the traditional system, but as soon as axes, chain saws and cash crops are introduced, the system breaks down with increasing field sizes and communications.

SECTION C

The painful transition

The transition from traditional subsistence to modern commercial farming is the equivalent of moving from the Stone Age to the 21st century in a generation. The effect on the ecosystem and the indigenous population is dramatic – often catastrophic and irreversible. An extreme example of this transition is provided by the recent history of the Panara (Kreen-Akarore) Indians of central Brazil.

Case study: The Panara of central Brazil

Until the early 1970s, little was known about this isolationist tribe. In 1961, the Panara had ambushed and killed a Cambridge geographer, who was a member of a Royal Geographical Society expedition to the region. Although small villages and unusual gardens were seen from the air, contact was not made until 1973, when work started on the building of the BR-165 Highway from Cuiabá (Mato Grosso) to Santarém (Amazonas). What happened to the Panara and their traditional homeland of the Rio Peixoto de Azevedo is unusual only in its pace, severity and positive outcome (8.2).

Initial contact with the external world led to the rapid introduction of diseases, including colds and influenza. Lacking any natural antibodies, the population was rapidly decimated, mainly by pneumonia, falling from an estimated 450 to 112 in less than a year.

Figure 8.2 Changes in the north of Mato Grosso between 1970 and 1990

Once the initial fear of white culture was overcome, the Panara drifted towards the new road, abandoning their villages and gardens. The fragmented tribe was unable to comprehend, let alone cope with, the 'road culture', and the remaining Panara were transferred to the

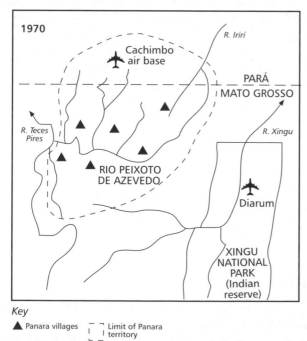

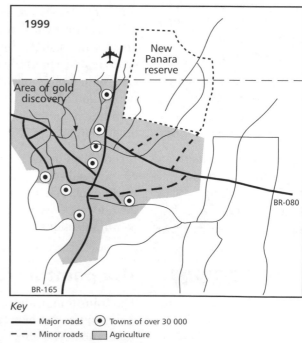

protected Xingu National Park within one year of initial contact. The road was completed by early 1975 and attracted the first wave of predominantly male settlers or pioneers, who cleared land, constructed housing and discovered gold in the sediments of the Peixoto valley.

A mini gold rush in the late 1970s rapidly increased the population and severely damaged the environment. The gold in river sands and gravel was most effectively removed by high-pressure water from hoses once the vegetation had been felled. This produced a lunar landscape of bare mounds of sand with pits. Mercury used to separate the gold also polluted the river and fish stocks were further depleted by the use of dynamite in fishing.

The Panara had been driven into this region in the early 19th century by European colonisation of the Mato Grosso. They had settled in a fertile area capable of sustaining their main crop of groundnuts (peanuts). With the much improved access afforded by the completed highway, however, commercial farmers were attracted to adjacent lands. By the end of the 1980s, a number of agribusinesses were established, with a large rural and urban population. The maps in **8.2** give some idea of the change that occurred in this area over little more than 20 years. In 1970, this region was rich virgin tropical rain forest; by 1990, it was an essentially rural landscape.

What makes this example unusual is that the indigenous people, the Panara, recovered, and after 15 years in the Xingu National Park they returned to an area near their traditional land. With the help of anthropologists, they gained title to their land. A rapid increase in population and a degree of assimilation of Western culture ensued. Today, the Panara are a flourishing and healthy community and yet retain much of their traditional lifestyle.

The sequence of initial isolation, abrupt contact, resource exploitation, colonisation and agricultural development is typical of tropical forest regions. It is disturbing to see an uncomprehending tribe suffering such uncontrollable and traumatic change, but the wider picture must also be considered. In 1970 the 450 Panara, with a subsistence economy, were occupying 58 100 km^2 of fertile land. Today, the same area is now inhabited by almost 350 000 Brazilians, who are contributing to the national economy. It is what happens to the region after colonisation that is the real issue and, in particular, whether the subsequent development is sustainable.

Review

4 Attempt to explain why the populations of indigenous tribes have remained static at low numbers. (It is suggested that you refer to the demographic transition model.)

5 Why is it so difficult for traditional and Western cultures to coexist?

6 Why did tribes such as the Panara require such large territories?

SECTION D

Pressures on the rain forest

The advertising slogan used in the 1970s by SUDAM, the development agency for the north of Brazil – 'Now is the time for the other half' – summarises the feeling of under-utilisation of Brazil's rain forest region. In Indonesia, the colonisation of Borneo and Timor was given the same positive image, namely that of helping national development through the economic integration of previously inactive regions. The immediate demand was for timber, agricultural produce and minerals. Such development of peripheral regions also served as a solution to problems elsewhere in the country. A highly simplified summary of the situation is shown in **8.3**, together with some of the forces fuelling the pressures. Many of the demands are mutually incompatible, all have some moral and economic justification, and there is no easy solution at local, national or international levels.

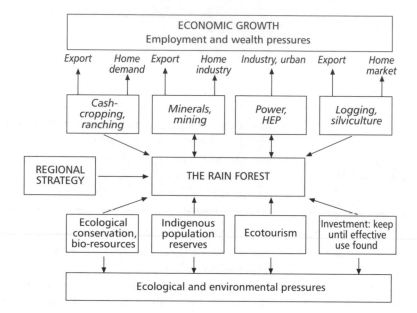

Figure 8.3 The main pressures on tropical rain forests

Logging

The large biomass gives a general perception that rain forests could sustain commercial forestry. Hardwood timber prices are high and the demand for woods such as mahogany, brazilwood, rosewood and green-heart for specialised uses remains high. After initial access, there is a short timber 'boom', but only for specific species that represent a relatively small fragment of the total tree volume (on average, less than 1 in 20). The valued trees are laboriously extracted and are generally exported as sawn timber. The dispersal of species makes logging difficult, as the distance between valuable trees is large. There are few concentrations to justify the construction of roads. The remaining wood has limited value, as it is unsuitable for the major market of pulp for paper manufacturing. In itself, the loss of some species is not critical, but the collateral damage to surrounding trees and the tracks used for access do have a devastating effect. Much of the burning that takes place as part of rain forest exploitation is because the wood has no commercial value. It is paradoxical that the reaction of Western consumers to this rape of the rain forests is to boycott tropical woods when, in economic terms, the most effective way to ensure conservation is to increase the value of the commodity. Logging is difficult to control and illegal extraction from the Amazon is estimated at £800 000 a year, with even greater losses from South-East Asia to supply the high demand for specialist woods in Japan (**8.4**).

Figure 8.4 The present status of humid tropical forests in selected countries, 1990

Country (area in 000 km²)	Primary forest cover		
	Original extent (000 km²)	Present extent (000 km²)	Current rate of deforestation (% per year)
Bolivia (1099)	90	45	2.1
Brazil (8512)	2860	1800	2.3
Central America (523)	500	55	3.7
Columbia (1139)	700	180	2.3
Congo (342)	100	80	0.8
Ecuador (271)	132	44	4.0
Indonesia (1919)	1220	530	1.4
Cote d'Ivoire (322)	160	4	15.6
Laos (237)	110	25	1.5
Madagascar (591)	62	10	8.3
Mexico (1967)	400	110	4.2
Nigeria (924)	72	10	14.3
Philippines (299)	250	8	5.4
Thailand (514)	435	22	8.4

Mineral extraction

Significant mineral reserves have been discovered in rain forest areas. The extensive lowlands of the Amazon, the Congo and Asia hold rich deposits of gold, precious stones, hydrated ores such as bauxite, cassiterite, as well as manganese and iron ore. In many cases, discovery has only been recent due to the general inaccessibility of areas. The radar surveying of Brazil (RADAM) from 1957 onwards has resulted in a significant expansion of known resources.

Mineral exploitation itself need not have a major impact on the rain forest environment, as mines are usually localised and processing is seldom on-site due to remoteness from energy supplies and markets. However, the impact is increased by the construction of transport routes (generally rail, due to the large volumes of material to be moved) and the supporting infrastructure of power, services and housing for the workforce. Any route offers a two-way flow and the result is often colonisation of the corridor along the route, and eventually the 'opening up' of entire regions.

There are examples of 'non-impact' resource development schemes, such as the manganese mine in Amapa Territory (northern Brazil) developed by the Bethlehem Steel Company. This has a very limited workforce and use of the railway is restricted. However, this is unusual and runs the risk of accusations that 'imperialism' is denying the locality the opportunity to develop its economy. Unorganised mineral developments have the greatest environmental impact, as usually accompanies the discovery of gold (see page 77). Individual fortune-seekers tend to have less environmental respect than publicly accountable companies, which also have the necessary capital and technology. At the Serra dos Pelados mine in Pará State (Brazil), the discovery of gold led to the *ad hoc* excavation of a giant pit with a temporary population of over 250 000 people (8.5). The devastation caused by spoil, refuse, mercury and deforestation was substantial. Mercifully, the mine was finally closed for safety reasons and the mining rights awarded to a company.

Figure 8.5 Mining at Serra dos Pelados

Case study: Serro dos Carajas

The resource development scheme of Serra dos Carajas is generally regarded as a working example of acceptable mineral extraction in a rain forest environment. High-grade iron ore (in excess of 65 per cent) was initially discovered in 1957. The mountain of iron ore, as well as copper and manganese, has since been worked by a transnational corporation (TNC) involving Japanese, American and European steel and oil companies. Providing 90 per cent of the total capital, skilled labour and technology, as well as monitoring of the local ecology, the TNC's involvement has helped set in motion a large, profitable and sustainable development. The scale of this project is vast and has involved the construction of a 'mine city' at Carajas, with an international airport, a good infrastructure, housing and services.

Fifty million tonnes of ore a year are transported to the coastal terminal at São Luis, along a custom-built 870 km railway. Power for the city, terminals and mine is provided by the massive Tucurui HEP plant that dams the adjacent Araguaia river. The total cost has been well in excess of £6 billion. An awareness of ecological impact has led to monitoring and research in the surrounding forests. Attempts have been made to reduce pollution from waste and emissions. The main problems have been secondary, through the arrival of uncontrolled migrants who have taken advantage of the improved accessibility of the area. This has triggered *ad hoc* activities, such as the 'gold pit' at Serra dos Pelados and, along the line of the railway, small-scale iron smelting using local charcoal. This latter activity has caused significant ecological damage and is proving difficult both to monitor and control.

Agriculture

The tropical humid climate offers great agricultural potential. The region has the highest NPP, suggesting high yields and multiple harvests, but attempts to realise this potential have met with very mixed fortunes. Four main types of agricultural practice have been tried.

Plantations

Initial attempts to exploit the humid Tropics commercially were through large estates or plantations, generally specialising in a specific crop. This organisation was introduced by Europeans, using a labour force initially of slaves and then of sharecroppers (labour that was paid by the right to work a small plot of land on the estate). In Asia, successful rubber plantations were established in Malaysia (**8.6**), but attempts at monocultivation of rubber in Brazil (the source of the *Hevea* species) failed through soil erosion and pests. In the north-east of Brazil, coastal rain forest had been successfully cleared for sugar cane and tobacco plantations, but their failure in Amazonas established the idea that this method could not be used in this climate. It was not until the 1970s, and the Jari Project by Daniel Ludwig, that successful large-scale monocultivation occurred in the Amazon Basin. This particular venture depended on high technology and pesticides to keep pests under control. Rice was planted on 14 000 ha of varzea (flood plain), giving yields ten times greater than the Brazilian average. The capital cost of the techniques used is extremely high, although the ability to produce two crops a year does illustrate the growth potential of the climate.

Ranching (savannaisation)

The global demand for meat is both large and consistent. Clearance, burning and grazing is a form of agriculture well suited to cheap land with a low population density. The new highways in Brazil have given access to large areas that were initially sold to agribusinesses for ranching. A similar use has occurred in Central America, stimulated by the high demand for meat in the USA. This land use only requires limited capital investment and a simple infrastructure; live cattle can be moved to market and the trade gains important hard currency.

In Brazil, ranches such as the Agro-Pecuaria Suia Missu (just to the east of the area in **8.2**) reach a scale of 700 000 ha and are financed by TNCs. These ranches only clear a fraction of their total area and cattle graze on unimproved pasture at a very low density. It has emerged that high subsidies are required, and that the land reverts to an infertile secondary scrub within ten years of initial clearance. If left, cleared rain forest areas regain 95 per cent of their biomass by weight within ten years, but many of the original species are lost. The taller trees tend not to re-grow, but are replaced by thorny, choking and extremely dense lower vegetation that is extremely costly to remove. This secondary succession is termed an **edaphic climax**, as primary species cannot re-establish in the depleted soil. A further criticism of this agricultural practice is that the large ranch strategy does not provide land or work for the landless population. The labour being shed by agricultural mechanisation in the south-east could not be absorbed.

Subsistence with cash-crop farming

This type of agriculture is more intensive and follows indigenous techniques. Small areas of land are allocated to colonists, who clear, burn and then cultivate a variety of subsistence and cash crops. In Brazil and Indonesia the governments allocate land, and such 'resettlement' schemes are socially and politically effective, providing low-cost solutions to a number of problems. They avoid the political problem of large estates, the landless rural population is given free land, there is a promise of increased food and cash-crop production, and there is some easing of the volume of rural–urban migration. However, the migrants to the rain forest environments are often given scant advice and guidance, although they come from regions with very different climates. Without assistance, they have difficulty in adapting to the new conditions. Forty per cent of the migrants to the Brazilian rain forest are from the north-east; their only knowledge is of how to cope with semi-arid conditions and drought.

Small-scale commercial farming

Medium-scale commercial farms, often organised through extended families or small companies, have been more successful. In Asia, $p\bar{a}d\bar{\imath}$ (paddy) rice cultivation in Java and Sumatra has provided a sustainable form of agriculture that is capable of supporting dense rural populations at a reasonable standard of living. Although the landscape is largely devoid of vegetation, the complex system of dykes and channels can control surface run-off and contain fluvial erosion. In Brazil, Japanese farmers in Pará State have established highly successful black pepper farms (now supplying 80 per cent of world production) using the techniques of tree-cropping. This involves cultivating crops of varying profitability that mimic the rain forest canopy and protect the surface. Even if fairly unproductive, the trees provide shade and shelter for the ground crops. Trees also

Figure 8.6 The organisation of rubber trees in a Malaysian plantation

increase soil fertility, with nitrogen-fixing species playing an important role, while the greater diversity of crops supports a larger range of micro-organisms that control pests. Tree-cropping requires knowledge, experience and a willingness to invest but, unfortunately, these attributes are rare among migrants entering the rain forest.

Silviculture (commercial forestry)

In natural rain forest systems, commercial forestry, or silviculture, has limited potential due to the dispersal of productive species. In 1967, Daniel Ludwig purchased the 1.2 million ha Jari Estate that had produced Brazil nuts. Over 75 000 ha of primary rain forest was cleared and planted with fast-growing tree species from Asia that were suitable for pulping. With a growth potential of up to 5 m a year and yielding 40 m³ per ha, these species were more productive than native trees. The scheme required a railway of over 200 km and, to process the wood, a floating pulp mill was constructed in Japan, towed to the River Jari and cemented into a constructed dock on the ranch. Kaolin was discovered locally, giving the pulp greater value. The success of this experiment in forest management is difficult to evaluate, as Ludwig was secretive. His supporters claim the forestry venture as a success and sustainable, while his critics claim expensive failure.

Conservation

Ecologists, environmentalists and anthropologists form a powerful and vociferous group demanding the protection of tropical forest areas. Their demands extend to maintaining the isolation of large areas of forest, thus preventing the influx of population and their use for agriculture or mineral extraction. The main mechanism has been the creation of parks and reserves, delineated areas with strict land-use controls, located in areas of particularly rich rain forest and low population density. In Brazil both national parks and conservation areas have been created (**8.7**), as well as Indian parks and reserves (**8.8**). These represent some 45 per cent of the Brazilian Amazon and, in theory, should preserve large tracts of forest. In practice, such designated areas are poorly funded, delineated and monitored, and management is often so ineffective as to allow invasion by settlers. To compound the problem, concentrations of Indian populations and rich forests tend to occur on the more fertile soils, and it is these that are under the greatest pressure for agricultural colonisation.

Park/reserve	Category	State	Year created	Area (ha)
Roraima*	National forest	Roraima	1989	2 664 685
Jaú	National park	Amazonas	1980	2 272 000
Pico da Neblina	National park	Amazonas	1979	2 200 000
Gorotire	Forest/resource reserve	Pará	1961	1 843 000
Serra do Araça	State park	Amazonas	1990	1 818 700
Tucumaque	Forest/resource reserve	Pará	1961	1 793 000
Parima	Forest/resource reserve	Roraima	1961	1 756 000
Amazonas	National forest	Amazonas	1989	1 573 100
Mundurucania	Forest/resource reserve	Pará	1961	1 377 000
Mamirauá	Ecological station	Amazonas	1990	1 124 000
Tefé	National forest	Amazonas	1989	1 020 000
Amazônia	National park	Amazonas/Pará	1974	993 500
Pacaás Novos	National park	Rondônia	1979	764 801
Taracua I	National forest	Amazonas	1990	674 400
Pari Cachoeira II	National forest	Amazonas	1989	654 000
Cabo Orange	National park	Amapá	1980	619 000
Piraiauara	National forest	Amazonas	1990	615 000
Serra do Divisor	National park	Acre	1989	605 000
Guaporé	Biological reserve	Rondônia	1982	600 000
Tapajós	National forest	Pará	1974	600 000
Rio Corumbiara	State park	Rondônia	1992	586 031
Araguaia	National park	Tocantins	1959	562 312
Uatuma	Biological reserve	Amazonas	1990	560 000
Taracua II	National forest	Amazonas	1990	559 504
Tarauacu II	National forest	Amazonas	1990	551 504
Igana-aiari	National forest	Amazonas	1990	491 300
Saracataquera	National forest	Pará	1989	429 600

Park/reserve	Category	State	Year created	Area (ha)
Cubate	National forest	Amazonas	1990	416 532
Amapa	National forest	Amapá	1989	412 000
Xie	National forest	Amazonas	1990	400 000
Lago Piratuba	Biological reserve	Amapá	1980	395 000
Caracaraí	Ecological station	Roraima	1982	394 560
Trombetas	Biological reserve	Pará	1979	385 000
Anavilhanas	Ecological station	Amazonas	1981	350 000
Gurupi	Biological reserve	Maranhão/Pará	1988	341 650
Mapia	National forest	Acre	1989	311 000
Jutai-Solimões	Ecological/biological	Amazonas	1983	288 187
Abufari	Biological reserve	Amazonas	1982	288 000
Niquia	Ecological station	Roraima	1985	286 600
Inauini-Teuini	National forest	Amazonas	1988	285 000
Bom Futuro	National forest	Rondonia	1988	280 000
Jaru	Biological reserve	Rondonia	1979	268 150
Guajara-Mirim	State park	Rondônia	1992	258 813
Purus	National forest	Amazonas	1988	256 000
Jari	Ecological station	Amapá/Pará	1982	227 126
Jamari	National forest	Rondônia	1984	215 000
Iquê	Ecological station	Mato Grosso	1981	200 000
Caxiuanã	National forest	Pará	1961	200 000
TOTAL				35 766 055

*Those shown in *italics* created after 1980.

Figure 8.7 Protected forest areas of over 200 000 ha in Brazil (1997)

Figure 8.8 Indian parks and reserves in Brazil (1998)

Situation	Number of lands	Area (ha)
To be identified	69	2 697 000
Being identified	91	5 049 463
Land-use restrictions	13	945 651
Delimited	47	17 695 825
Reserved or demarcated	15	74 966
Confirmed	66	17 278 964
Registered	262	58 384 427
TOTAL	563	102 126 296

7 Explore ways of reducing the global demand for rain forest hardwoods.

8 Write a short analytical report based on the data in **8.4**. Illustrate your report with appropriate maps and diagrams.

9 To what extent do you agree with the view that mineral exploitation need not adversely affect the rain forest?

10 Assess the relative merits of the four types of agricultural practice.

11 Do you think that commercial forestry has a future in the humid Tropics?

12 Explain why the designation of parks and reserves does not necessarily guarantee the future of the rain forest.

SECTION E

Is sustainable development possible in the rain forest?

In the short term, exploiting the rain forests contributes hard currency through export to feed the domestic population and support industrial expansion. In addition, the development of these sparsely populated areas is a potential solution to the problems of **regional disparity**. Third World countries such as Indonesia and Brazil are frequently characterised by an uneven distribution of wealth and population. They have their **core regions** containing a high proportion of the urban population, services and industry, while **peripheral regions** are rural, poor and lack both infrastructure and industry. The disparity is a major cause of selective migration that, in turn, causes greater disparity. The rain forest areas represent regions of **under-population**, as there are too few people to exploit the resources of the area, while areas such as the north-east of Brazil are **over-populated**, with a population that is too large for the resource base. The construction of roads, moving the capital to Brasilia and allocating free land have allowed the Brazilian government effectively to 'guide' population from areas of surplus to areas of deficit. Such a strategy has the potential to reduce over-population and slow the growth of the overcrowded cities of the south-east. In this respect, pressure on the rain forests must be placed in a wider context of national economic and demographic trends, as well as what is best in the national interest.

There have been agricultural success stories, including rubber plantations, *pādī* rice and tree-cropping in Asia and black pepper cultivation in Brazil. These indicate that certain requirements are needed in order to make agriculture sustainable:

■ The scheme should ensure that colonists are made aware of the problems inherent in rain forest environments.

- The scheme should be well resourced and monitored, so that if degradation threatens it can be rectified at an early point. This requires high technology and specialist labour.
- Profits and subsidies should be controlled to discourage short-term strategies when land is abandoned after a limited use, as it is more profitable to buy and clear new land than to maintain or manage the old.
- Companies and individuals should be made responsible for the environmental consequences of their actions.
- A comprehensive knowledge of areas is required before planning decisions are taken. Areas with fertile soils and high-grade minerals should be released for development, but areas with lower-quality soils should be left untouched. Preserved areas must be large and continuous, as small areas do not contain the range of species required for ecosystems to function properly.

The main problem is that the resources required for the sensitive development of tropical rain forests are generally not available in the less-developed countries (LEDCs) where the forests occur. Those resources are in the more-developed countries (MEDCs) of the temperate world. But the latter have a history of extensive environmental modification, including widespread deforestation. The colonial powers amongst them have an even greater record of deforestation in tropical and sub-tropical areas. So this raises the question of why the loss of rain forest appears to be such an issue with the MEDCs. Why should today's LEDCs not be allowed to follow the path that was originally trodden by MEDCs? The questions can be addressed at two levels, as follows.

National
- A unique natural resource is being destroyed for low, short-term gains when a long-term strategy could yield far greater rewards.
- The changes to the local hydrological cycle will cause regional climatic change, with the 'green hell' becoming a 'red desert'.
- This will cause a significant increase in surface run-off, fluvial erosion and the loss of soil. More extreme river regimes will cause sedimentation of existing reservoirs.
- Higher peak discharges will increase flood risks.
- The colonists will be left impoverished and will require new and costly government intervention.
- Large-scale burning causes severe local smoke pollution and exposed dry surfaces produce dust storms.

International
- The tropical rain forest basins provide a core component of the global atmospheric system. Reduced vegetation converts less carbon dioxide into oxygen, and changes in atmospheric water vapour and the modified albedo of the surface have direct implications for global weather. These systems are too complex for the precise knock-on effect to be calculated with any degree of accuracy.

- The rain forests form the largest and least researched gene pool left on Earth. The flora, fauna and indigenous populations almost certainly hold material of considerable scientific value, both in humanitarian and commercial applications. Of the estimated 10 million species in the world, 27 000 are lost each year (three per hour) and a significant proportion of these were in the rain forests.
- Carbon dioxide released by the burning contributes to global warming, as it absorbs out-going long-wave radiation in the greenhouse effect.
- Tropical rain forests provide a unique and rich ecosystem that should be accessible to future generations.

Large-scale deforestation has historical precedents and attitudes tend to reflect the interests of the observer. Environmental groups are increasingly well organised and are able to influence events through pressure on the organisations involved in projects. Conversely, business groups remain willing to make substantial investments in one of the last remaining frontiers, and LEDC governments continue to see the 'taming' of the rain forest as a matter of national pride and integration.

Figure 8.9 Projected land use in the Brazilian Amazon

Type of land use	Estimated area (million ha)	% of total area
Areas cleared for non-forestry purposes	78.8	30.3
Areas cleared for agricultural purposes	40.0	15.4
Natural pasturage	15.0	5.8
Flood plains, swamps and mangroves	9.5	3.7
Indian reserves	20.0	7.7
National parks and biological reserves	43.0	16.5
'Sustained-yield' forest reserves	53.7	20.7
TOTAL AREA	260.0	100.0

To be realistic, the outlook for the rain forest is somewhat bleak in that further reduction of its extent is inevitable, although much of this will be in the drier fringes. Pressure is most intense in South-East Asia (**8.4**) with more cores of economic development, islands allowing penetration into forest interiors and dynamic rates of population growth that intensify the pressure on forests. In Africa, population and economic growth are slowing and therefore reducing pressure on forest areas. In the Amazon Basin, the sheer scale offers some protection and even after three decades of deforestation large tracts remain intact (**8.9**). With a slowing rate of population increase and increasing ecological awareness, it is to be hoped that significant and meaningful areas will be effectively protected. The core of the Amazon forest is currently protected as it forms the periphery of eight countries, but with greater economic integration it would become the core to them all. Much may also depend on Western attitudes and their willingness to assume a greater and more practical role in saving the rain forests for the future of the planet.

Review

13 Why did extensive deforestation in Europe not result in land degradation?

14 What are the characteristics of Third World economies that increase the difficulties of ever achieving a sustainable use of rain forest environments?

15 What is meant by the term **sustainable development**?

16 As a resident in a more-developed country, why do you think that the conservation of rain forests matters?

17 Why might residents of a less-developed country favour deforestation and development?

18 What practical assistance could more-developed countries offer to help conserve the rain forests?

19 Outline recent major demographic and economic changes that offer greater hope for the rain forests.

20 With your fellow students, debate the motion that 'Countries have a right to use their national resources in a way that they see fit, regardless of international implications.'

Enquiry

1 With reference to a named indigenous group practising traditional agricultural techniques in a tropical rain forest environment:
   a identify the ways in which the traditional methods may be considered as sustainable
   b outline the disadvantages of such a system of agricultural production
   c draw an annotated nutrient cycle to show what occurs during a slash-and-burn agricultural cycle.

2   Select one region of rain forest that is under threat.
  a Draw a map to show the location of the forest, the main roads and the settlements, and identify the main types of pressure occurring in the region.
  b Compile a report justifying a scheme of colonisation and forest clearance (describe and explain the potential benefits of the scheme).
  c Write a critique of the scheme (describe and explain the potentially negative effects of the development).

3   From books, articles or the Internet, research one mineral exploitation scheme that has occurred in a tropical forest environment.
  a Draw a map to show the location of the mineral resource, the links to markets, the infrastructure associated with the development and the settlements.
  b Annotate the map to show the main elements of environmental impact.
  c Outline the main advantages of your scheme for the region and the country.
  d Examine the main criticisms of the scheme and how are these being managed by the company concerned
  e To what extent can the mineral exploitation be considered as less environmentally damaging than agriculture?

9

The way forward?

The impact of human activity on natural systems is now so severe that it has become a major global concern. Acid rain, global warming, ozone holes and rising sea levels are human impacts that are beginning to invite global disaster. Development is an almost irrepressible process, but there is now a growing pressure for it to assume a much more sustainable form. Development should not be allowed to result in net losses; materials or energy consumed should be replaced or replenished. There is a need for people throughout the world to reach that state of equilibrium in which development continues but without serious depletion of the globe's finite resources. Sustainability may be a new 'buzz' word that slips easily into conversations, but its application to tropical environments is far from straightforward.

Wilderness regions

The environmental constraints imposed by either extremely high or very low precipitation have prevented large-scale human occupation of tropical forests and deserts, so that many remain sparsely populated with untouched landscapes. That situation is now threatened by a human activity not yet considered in this book. Transport developments, increasing incomes and leisure time and a better awareness of the natural world have led to a new pressure: international tourism. In the present context, it is the desire of many people living in temperate latitudes to experience tropical environments while they still exist.

The term **wilderness** refers to areas where human activity has not had a significant impact on the landscape. Such areas are typically remote, and have low population densities and limited economic potential. Wilderness is relative and can be used at any geographical scale. Globally, it refers to areas such as the Antarctic, Greenland and the Himalayas, as well as tropical rain forests and hot deserts. At a regional scale, areas such as the Lake District in England or Snowdonia in North Wales may be considered as wildernesses in contrast to the prevailing urban and agricultural landscapes. At a local scale, an isolated area of woodland or scrub may be described as a wilderness, as natural processes have started to dominate over human order. The importance of wilderness in a geographical context is that it gives an insight into how landscape would look without the scars of human intervention.

The concept of wilderness can be questioned, as it seems likely that all areas of the world have at some stage been affected by human activities. Logically, tropical rain forests have all been modified by slash-and-burn horticulture or hunting–gathering, even where population is very sparse. In the Amazon, 10 000 years of slash-and-burn horticulture must have affected plant and animal species through the introduction of new crops and the selective felling and burning of trees. The Nazca Lines in the Atacama Desert of Peru are visible from space and were created by a sparse population in one of the most hostile deserts in the world.

Once areas left untouched through lack of interest, wilderness regions have now become an issue and are increasingly protected by legislation. The reasons why areas of 'nothingness' should be protected include the following:

- They provide a record of how the world once was and in this sense are irreplaceable.
- Their flora and fauna can survive as natural systems for future study and possible use, as well as providing a gene pool for the future.
- They provide an educational resource for an increasingly urban population.
- They are fragile and easily disrupted by any human activity.
- We owe it to future generations that we preserve unique areas.

Counter-arguments to those just given include the following:

- The entire Earth was once a wilderness, and it is unreasonable to disadvantage less-developed countries.
- Preservation of tropical wilderness regions represents imperialism in a new form and prevents LEDCs from utilising their resources.
- The increasing demand for resources has already reached the point at which it is unreasonable to leave large areas untouched.
- With changes in global climate and atmosphere (largely caused by MEDCs), there are no true natural environments left.
- Countries have a right to exploit their territory as they wish, without control by the international community.

The pressures on wilderness regions have no solution that satisfies all parties (**9.1**). Wilderness regions have to be fairly large, as the concept implies embracing functioning physical systems with a full range of flora and fauna. Such wilderness regions also need buffer zones to reduce the impact of adjacent modified environments. In situations in which species migrate, one wilderness region may even depend on the maintenance of another wilderness region in a reciprocal relationship.

The complexity of conflicts over wilderness regions can be illustrated by the Naua, who inhabit a remote area of rain forest in the Brazilian State of Acre. Protection through remoteness was lost with the construction of the BR-364 Highway and the Naua were rediscovered after being thought extinct. Under Brazilian law, the Naua have an automatic right to

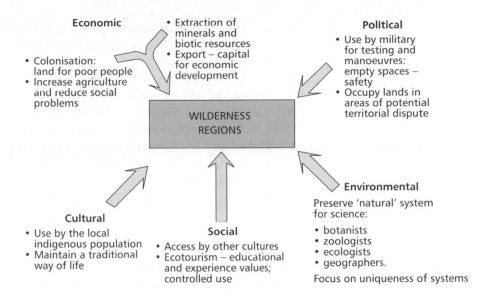

Figure 9.1 Conflict over wilderness regions

Economic
- Colonisation: land for poor people
- Increase agriculture and reduce social problems

- Extraction of minerals and biotic resources
- Export – capital for economic development

Political
- Use by military for testing and manoeuvres: empty spaces – safety
- Occupy lands in areas of potential territorial dispute

WILDERNESS REGIONS

Environmental
Preserve 'natural' system for science:
- botanists
- zoologists
- ecologists
- geographers.

Focus on uniqueness of systems

Cultural
- Use by the local indigenous population
- Maintain a traditional way of life

Social
- Access by other cultures
- Ecotourism – educational and experience values; controlled use

demarcated land, but the area had already been demarcated as a national park. Thus the Naua could be forced to move to a new territory, as 'no humans are allowed to live in such environmentally sensitive areas'.

Review

1 Why are some areas of the world untouched by human activity?

2 Summarise the main arguments for preserving wilderness areas.

3 Summarise the main arguments for exploiting resources in wilderness areas.

4 With reference to a specific wilderness area, identify the main pressure groups that have an interest in it.

Ecotourism

Ecotourism potentially allows access to exotic environments while providing local employment with low environmental impact. This seems to offer the hope of satisfying international demands for protection while meeting national demands of employment, wealth and development.

The term **ecotourism** was first coined by Lash in 1987, but lacks a precise definition and is used to refer to a range of activities that share a number of characteristics:

■ It is a voluntary activity during leisure time, generally considered as a 'holiday'. The purpose of the visit is personal satisfaction rather than economic gain.

- The area visited is 'natural', as the environment has not been significantly modified by people, and it will include both physical and cultural components.
- There is an element of 'danger' or personal discomfort, and the experience will be new to the individual.
- The visitors do not disturb the area by their presence and the activity is sustainable, with minimal impact on the environment.
- The visitors learn from the experience through instruction or contact with indigenous groups, and their understanding and knowledge of the environment are increased.
- The activity is run, controlled by or assisted by the local population rather than imposed on the area by external commercial concerns.

Traditional activities such as hunting safaris contrast with ecotourism, as they impose external values and often devastate the environment. Modern safaris are considered to be ecotourism, as the 'hunting' is carried out using a camera and the impact on the local environment is controlled. Ecotourism has a label of respectability and responsibility, and allows MEDC populations access to exotic environments without the stigma of interference. However, this concept is inherently ethnocentric and imperialistic, as the activity is on the terms and conditions of the MEDCs, which provide the tourists, rather than on those of the host culture. Contact with 'no change' is a crucial ingredient, allowing waves of visitors to experience the untouched environment, but this does not take into account the hopes and aspirations of the local populations. A fundamental assumption of the sustainability model is that the host population does not want to change. But this ignores the fact that the attraction of ecotourism for local people in the destination area is to gain wealth in order to change and develop. The local populations have their own ideas about the benefits of ecotourism and these are often in contrast to those of the visitor.

Case study: The humid Tropics (Amazonas)

Since the 15th century, the tropical rain forests have presented a powerful image of nature. They combine luxuriant vegetation, exotic flora and fauna with an indigenous population that has strange customs and is seemingly in harmony with its environment. Increasingly seen as 'guardians of nature', they have received international recognition though eco-schemes such as that of 'The Body Shop'. The retailer's use of naturally occurring forest products in cosmetics was intended to help the forest dwellers in a sustainable manner. In the West, the rain forest is perceived as an environment that defeats people, with an economic history characterised by failure. As a destination for tourists, it provides the ultimate contrast with the order of urban life, offering a unique and adventurous experience.

Figure 9.2 Manaus – at the heart of the forest. Amazonas as presented on a ecotourism website

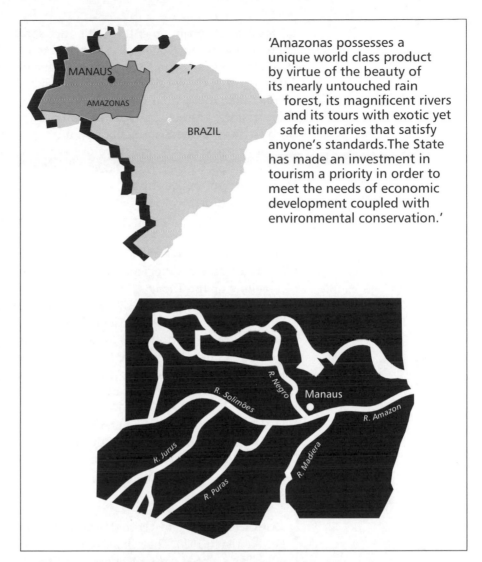

'Amazonas possesses a unique world class product by virtue of the beauty of its nearly untouched rain forest, its magnificent rivers and its tours with exotic yet safe itineraries that satisfy anyone's standards. The State has made an investment in tourism a priority in order to meet the needs of economic development coupled with environmental conservation.'

In Brazil, ecotourism is a well-established significant economic activity. Located at the junction of the Rio Negro and the Amazon (**6.5**), the city of Manaus (population 1.5 million) has an international airport, road links, hotels and service facilities, and is located in the centre of a large area of relatively undisturbed rain forest (**9.2**). In 1993, 72 tour operators were offering eco-related packages ranging in duration from half a day to several weeks. These are organised by EMAMTUR, the Tourists Board of Amazonas State, and are mainly concentrated within 150 km of the city. Access to the sites is by small boat or along the generally unpaved roads. Ecotourists are generally housed in lodges that are often floating, small, built from local materials, run by local people, use low technology and offer few comforts to visitors.

The Amazon Lodge is a typical example. Built as a floating raft, it employs 14 people and handles a maximum of 2000 visitors a year, with no more than 40 at any one time. Access to the forest is 'natural'; there are no trails and canoe trips rotate different routes to reduce the impact on the riverine environment. Facilities are spartan with no air-conditioning or hot water; all refuse is taken to the nearest town and food is from local sources. Visitors are educated in the structure and functioning of the local ecosystems but, like all Amazonian ecotours, contact with indigenous people is limited to **cobocolos** (local 'frontiersmen') rather than Amerindian groups. The cultural element is a problem, as indigenous Amerindians are vulnerable to both disease and economic exploitation, and therefore are protected against uncontrolled access. Culture as such is provided by visits to museums and to some of the historic enterprises of the region, such as the abandoned Ford rubber plantations (**9.3**).

Figure 9.3 Two 'Amazon Tours'

> ### Fordlândia – 3 Days and 3 nights
> Leave Santarém by regional riverboat at pre-scheduled time. Before travelling up the Tapajós River visit the 'meeting of the waters', where the Amazon and Tapajós Rivers come together. Arrive in Alter do Chão before mid-day. Visit the Museum of Indigenous Art, lunch onboard boat and continue upstream to Aramanai. Visit the only active rubber tree plantation in the region. Dinner and sleep aboard. Arrive in Fordlândia before noon on second day. Tour village and the old industrial plant in the afternoon. Sleep aboard riverboat in Fordlândia.
>
> Day 3, begin journey back to Santarém. The boat will moor at one of the beautiful sandy beaches of the Tapajós River the last evening. Arrive in Santarém at approximately 7:30 AM the next day. For persons with early morning flights, arrangements can be made for the boat to arrive earlier.
>
> Historical Note: Henry Ford (Ford Motor Company) founded Fordlândia in 1928. The rubber tree plantation was active until 1946, when Ford closed down all operations, including the larger Belterra plantation. Secluded geographically from most of the world, it is truly a living museum of a past history.

> ### Bosque Santa Lúcia – 3 to 4 hours
> Bosque Santa Lúcia (Santa Lúcia Woods) is an excellent choice for seeing upland flora. Begin the excursion in Santarém from the deep-water pier located on the Tapajós River. Continue south on the Santarém–Cuiabá Highway, the only road connecting this part of the Amazon with other points in Brazil. We will reach an elevation of 158 meters (518 feet), which might be considered the Alps of the Amazon. A few minutes later we will enter a secondary dirt road that will take us to Bosque Santa Lúcia. Different stages of 'slash and burn' agriculture and the effect it has on the forest and land can be observed on this stretch of road.

At Bosque Santa Lúcia your guide will choose one of more than 5 kilometers (3 miles) of trails for that nature walk you have wanted to take since arriving in the Amazon. As you stroll over the forest trails you will have the opportunity to fraternize with biodiversity. More than 400 different species of regional trees are to be found at Bosque Santa Lúcia, some examples of which have been labelled for your convenience. Although a secondary forest, Bosque Santa Lúcia provides most of the characteristics noted throughout the more distant, inaccessible virgin forest, that is, widely diversified species of trees and plants making use of nutrient-poor tropical soils. Discover for yourself the secrets of how they manage.

The inclusion of Belterra and Fordlândia as ecotours is curious, as both were attempts to introduce plantation agriculture to the Amazon, with disastrous consequences. The emphasis is on the futility of plantation techniques in such an environment, and is attractive to ecotourists from the USA.

Case study: The arid Tropics (Ayers Rock, Australia)

Ayers Rock has geographical fame as the largest single surface rock and is also regarded as a model of successful ecotourism. Ayers Rock is remote, near the centre of Australia (**9.4**), and in a hostile and sparsely populated desert. The area was an Aboriginal reserve, but was taken over by the Australian government for development as a tourist and wildlife reserve in 1958. By 1968, developments to cope with the 23 000 visitors a year had made a significant environmental impact, with an airstrip, hotels and services located adjacent to the rock. Waste disposal, water supply and soil erosion were all becoming problems and the site was increasingly unsustainable.

Following a critical report in 1972, the village was moved 20 km from the Rock and reopened in 1983 as Uluru Village. It was designed to minimise environmental damage (**9.5**). Ownership of the Uluru–Kata Tjuta National Park was returned to the Aboriginal tribes, who now run the reserve jointly with the Australian Nature Conservation Agency. The policy aims to meet the needs of both the tourists and the local Aboriginal population. In 1987, the Rock was given World Heritage Site status and by 1993 it was receiving over 250 000 visitors a year.

The spatial separation of the Rock and the resort allows the provision of accommodation and facilities for visitors without impinging on the natural setting of the former. Educational facilities inform tourists about the Aboriginal way of life and the status of the Rock as a highly sacred site. Local people acting as guides on walks further teach visitors about

Figure 9.4 The location of Ayers Rock

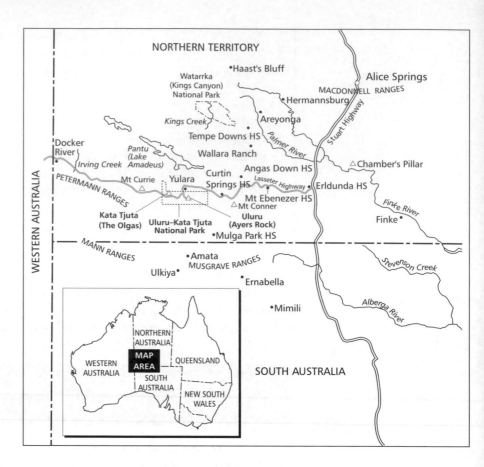

Figure 9.5 Uluru Village

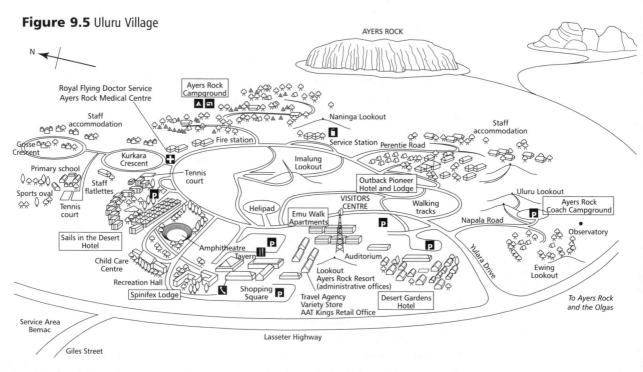

their own culture and traditions (**9.6**). Access to the Rock is by coach, and there is an entry fee that contributes towards the development and the local people. Friction still occurs over tourists wanting to walk on the Rock (the Aborigines themselves will not do this) and over how much further expansion should occur. In general, the current development is sustainable, as the ecotourists have a unique experience, the indigenous culture is not compromised and the environment is not significantly damaged.

Figure 9.6 A tour itinerary at Ayers Rock

Review

5 What do the outline itineraries in Amazonas tell you about ecotourism?

6 What kind of impact are such tours likely to have on the environment?

7 Identify the main types of people likely to be attracted by ecotourism.

8 Outline the problems likely to be created by ecotourism on the scale of the Ayers Rock example.

9 Examine the particular problems posed by the physical environment for ecotourism in:

■ tropical rain forest areas
■ hot arid environments.

Ranger-guided Mala Walk (daily)
8.00 am October–April (inclusive)
10.00 am May–September (inclusive)
Meet the Ranger at the Mala Walk sign at the base of Uluru. The walk is a great opportunity to learn about the Aboriginal perceptions of Uluru, its powerful spiritual significance and how Anangu Traditional Owners and Rangers are looking after the Park together. There are many fine examples of Anangu art to see along the way. The walk finishes at Kantju Gorge. Allow approx. 1.5 hrs. The tour is free and the track is wheelchair accessible.

Cultural Centre Tour
This tour of the Cultural Centre is led by Anangu Rangers. It gives you the opportunity to meet Pitjantjatjara and Yankunytjatjara speakers and to learn about Tjukurpa (Anangu law and creation time), and managing an Aboriginal National Park. You also gain an insight into the Anangu enterprises in the park.

Meet at the Cultural Centre Information Desk. The free tour is conducted Monday, Tuesday and Wednesday afternoons only. Please ask the Information Officer to confirm your place and starting time.

Although involving strongly contrasting environments, both of these examples share the common problem of environmental fragility. The challenge of balancing access and involvement for tourists with sustainability and low environmental impact is demanding. This is mainly because the relationship between flora, fauna and soil is extremely sensitive and is easily disturbed. At Ayers Rock, the remoteness presents problems for access, with an ever increasing number of flights, and also for waste disposal, energy, water supplies and vehicle access. Although lessened by the spatial separation of the settlement, footpath erosion, climbing on the rock and the disturbance of fauna remain problematical. In the rain forest, the movement of tourists by road and river, the construction of forest trails and problems of waste disposal and energy production serve to increase costs and reduce scale and thus profit. It is difficult to maintain a wilderness and at the same time allow visitors in.

Is ecotourism sustainable?

Ecotourism derives its sustainability from limiting the impact of tourists on local human and physical environments, but its long-term viability remains unclear. Traditional models of tourism (**9.7**) show a pattern of increase followed by decline; a pattern that is all too common in the 'boom and bust' economic history of arid and humid tropical regions. The initial increase in tourism reflects spreading knowledge and the improvement of marketing, access and facilities. The decline occurs when the area becomes over-exploited, is regarded as 'commonplace' or the attraction itself becomes unfashionable. Ecotourism appears to be extremely vulnerable, as one of its main attractions is the 'unusual' – an experience that is not shared with many other people. In effect, canoeing on the Amazon and walking through the rain forest is only an experience if few other people have done it.

Figure 9.7 The product model of tourism

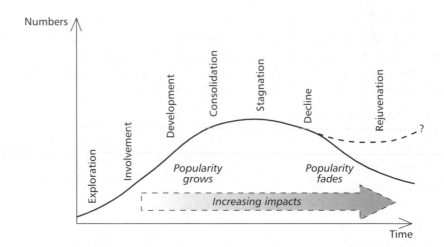

The current scale of many ecotourism ventures is probably sustainable provided that the environments concerned remain fashionable, but the generation of capital and employment is not particularly great. The Amazon Lodge only caters for 2000 visitors a year and employs 14 people, yet it requires several hundred square kilometres of forest and river. For tourism to provide an economic base, the scale has to increase. This means catering for a more demanding clientele that will expect home comforts, recognisable food, easier access and entertainment. At this point, the central tenets of ecotourism are likely to break down, and the short-term strategy will lead to longer-term decline, environmental degradation and the movement of ecotourism to new, unspoilt areas. The proposal to build a large resort hotel complex near Manaus, catering for large groups arriving by charter flights, suggests that ecotourism in Brazil is already starting to develop in a more commercial direction. The success and commercialisation of the Parana Ecological Trail in the south-east of Brazil shows how genuine ecotourism can develop into a mass tourist venture under the pressures of profit, employment and regional development.

10 With reference to the tourism product cycle (9.7), explain why the number of ecotourists is likely to grow.

11 How might this growth contribute to later decline?

12 What, if anything, might be done to help prevent possible decline?

13 Which environment do you think is most threatened – the hot desert or the rain forest? Give your reasons.

14 Identify one area of tropical forest and one area of hot desert that you think will still be untouched in 50 years' time. Justify your choices.

Therefore, in conclusion, it seems that ecotourism offers a potentially sustainable economic activity for both tropical rain forests and arid lands, but it can only be expected to make a limited contribution to the broader development process. Not all arid and humid tropical areas have the sorts of feature that interest and attract ecotourists. Furthermore, the ecotourist market probably has a limited capacity. To comprehend and understand these environments requires a specialist education, and it is difficult to see how an expensive vacation with difficult access and demanding local conditions will ever attract tourism on a commercially viable scale. Ecotourism may well serve to increase the awareness of an important segment of the world's more-developed population, but as a long-term solution to employment and development in remote regions, it is unlikely to play an important role without pressing the 'self-destruct' button.

Enquiry

1 Using the Internet and referring to books and articles, identify one example of ecotourism in a hot desert environment and one in the tropical rain forest. To what extent do your examples meet the requirements of ecotourism in terms of:
   a treatment of the environment
   b involvement of local people
   c types of activity
   d type of accommodation?

2 Select a tropical rain forest or a hot desert area that is currently not an ecotourist destination.
   a Design and produce a one-page advertisement for a proposed venture in the area, giving details of accommodation and ethical conduct.
   b Produce a map to show the location of the area and its attractions.
   c What problems might you face in trying to start an ecotourism venture in your chosen area?
   d Why might local people be suspicious of your motives?

Further reading and resources

The humid and arid tropics are included in most general AS/A2 geography textbooks and there are also numerous specialised books available. In addition, these environments are well represented on the Internet, with more up-to-date information and excellent images.

General reading

Andrew Goudie, *The Nature of the Environment*, fourth edition, Blackwell, 2001 (also updated).

Andrew Goudie, *The Human Impact on the Natural Environment*, fifth edition, Blackwell, 2000.

Brian Knapp, Simon Ross and D. McCrae, *Challenge of the Natural Environment*, Longman, 1989.

David Waugh, *Geography, an Integrated Approach*, third edition, Nelson Thornes, 2000.

Specialised

Andrew Goudie and John Wilkinson, *The Warm Desert Environment*, Cambridge University Press, 1977.

Ronald L. Heathcote, *The Arid Lands: their Use and Abuse*, Longman, 1983.

Paul W. Richards, *The Tropical Rain Forest: an Ecological Study*, second edition, Cambridge University Press, 1996.

Timothy C. Whitmore, *An Introduction to the Tropical Rain Forests*, second edition, Clarendon Press, 1998.

Websites

Specific site addresses change, so try searching for the following and then exploring the site menus:

http://www.nasa.gov – a large and excellent collection of images and text. Look for the Goddard Centre (Goddard from Space) and Geomorphology from Space sites.

http://www.inpe.br (Instituto Nacional de Pesquisas Espaciais) – a Brazilian site with excellent aerial images of the rainforest, that clearly show the extent and evolution of deforestation.

http://www.worldclimate.com – a site that gives extensive climatic data for selected locations.